Jerusalem's
GATES

Illustrating the
Christian Life

Jerusalem's GATES

Illustrating the
Christian Life

IAN TAYLOR

ECS
MINISTRIES
The Word to the World

Jerusalem's Gates
Ian Taylor

Published by:
ECS Ministries
PO Box 1028
Dubuque, IA 52004-1028
phone: (563) 585-2070
email: ecsorders@ecsministries.org
website: www.ecsministries.org

First Printed 2005 (AK '05) 1 Unit
Reprinted 2009 (AK '05) 1 Unit
Reprinted 2013 (AK '05) 1 Unit

Copyright © 2005 ECS Ministries

ISBN 978-1-59387-042-3

Code: B-JG

Printed in the United States of America

CONTENTS

FOREWORD

There is a great need today for training in how to live the Christian life. Many of us look for suitable devotional material to hand to new believers to ground them in the essentials necessary for growth. Ian Taylor's spiritual insights into Nehemiah's reconstruction of Jerusalem's gates provide the kind of material we need.

The tour around Jerusalem with a stop at each gate provides an illustration of Christian living. The Sheep Gate reminds us that Jesus is the Lamb of God. The Fish Gate reminds of that we need to be fishers of men. The Old Gate reminds us that there is much value in the old paths. The Valley Gate can form a picture of our need to develop humility. The Dung Gate reminds us of our need for spiritual purity. The Fountain Gate can speak of the filling of the Spirit. The Water Gate represents the importance of the Word of God. The Horse Gate can illustrate Christian warfare. The East Gate symbolizes the hope of Messiah's return. And the Inspection Gate reminds us of the coming judgment.

Each chapter is suitable for a day's devotional study. It is written in an easily understood style. The best approach would be to give this book to a new Christian disciple, suggest he read it a chapter at a time, and then meet to discuss the subject introduced in the reading. Plan to answer questions and delve more deeply into some of the passages suggested. May the Lord use this book to help us teach disciples how to follow Christ.

Ken Daughters
President, Emmaus Bible College
Dubuque, Iowa

INTRODUCTION

Setting the Scene

The book of Nehemiah transports us back to a fascinating time in Jewish history. About 150 years before the events chronicled by Nehemiah, the Babylonians under King Nebuchadnezzar crushed the troublesome little kingdom of Judah and carried off most of its survivors to Babylon.

The years of captivity in Babylon were the result of the Jews' disobedience to God and their constant rejection of his laws, especially those concerning idolatry (Jeremiah 25:1-13). The Jews had been pulled into idolatrous worship of the gods of the pagan nations surrounding them.

God had determined that the Jewish captivity would last seventy years. At the appointed time, Cyrus (king of Persia at that time) fulfilled the prophecies of Isaiah and Jeremiah, decreeing in 538 BC that the Jews were free to return to Jerusalem (see 2 Chronicles 36:22; Isaiah 44:28; 45:1, 13; Jeremiah 25:11-13). It would take many decades, however, to reestablish the Jewish nation in their homeland. Just over 40,000 Jews returned with Cyrus's written command to rebuild the temple (Ezra 2:64). They encountered fierce opposition from the Samaritans, who hindered the rebuilding of the temple for a number of years. With God's encouragement through his prophetic messengers Haggai ("Build My temple!") and Zechariah ("Don't be afraid, you are My people!"), the temple was finally rebuilt.

About fifty years after this second temple was completed, Ezra, a godly priest and scribe, set out from Persia with a group of about 5,000 Jews, including many priests and Levites, to facilitate the temple service (Ezra 8). At this time the Jews began to reestablish themselves as a nation. With the temple rebuilt and the priests functioning in their roles, the fullness of Jewish religious life was finally reestablished. The people, however, were still vulnerable to enemy attacks, due to the fact that the city walls stood in ruins. In order to provide security and protection for its citizens, the walls of Jerusalem needed to be rebuilt.

Nehemiah—The King's Cupbearer and God's Building Supervisor

From the first chapter of the book of Nehemiah, we begin to understand the type of man whom God would use to remedy Jerusalem's vulnerability. We see that Nehemiah was trustworthy; he was the cupbearer to the king, and the one whom the king trusted daily with his life. He knew the Scriptures and was a man of prayer. It is a profitable exercise to read through the book, taking special note of the many times Nehemiah prayed.

One day, while in the fortress city of Susa, Nehemiah's brother Hanani brought troubling news from Jerusalem that the newly reestablished nation was in peril for lack of defenses. He told Nehemiah about Jerusalem's ruined walls and of the people's fear. Nehemiah began to pray day and night, reminding God of his covenant to bless and care for his people, who now sought to obey and worship him.

Later, while Nehemiah was serving the king wine, the king noticed Nehemiah's distressed state and asked what was troubling him. Nehemiah told of his worry for his people in Jerusalem. "What is it you want?" asked the king. Nehemiah quickly prayed and then set forth his request: "If it pleases the king and if your servant has found favor in his sight, let him send me to the city in Judah where my fathers are buried so that I can rebuild it" (Nehemiah 2:5).

This wish was granted, and Nehemiah set off for Jerusalem with a clear understanding of his mission in God's service.

On his arrival, Nehemiah took the opportunity to ride around the wall alone one evening to personally gather information about its deteriorated condition. He then felt free to inform the Jews of the nature of his visit. He began to organize his fellow Jews for the work. During the huge construction project, Nehemiah stood firm despite the many obstacles and opponents that came his way. He did not allow himself to become discouraged, acting instead with much wisdom and decisiveness—even when the Samaritans sought to take his life.

Viewing the Gates and Walls of Jerusalem through Spiritual Eyes

The third chapter of Nehemiah describes the construction of the wall and its ten gates. God's Word records the eternal testimonies of those who helped and those who did not. The chapter details the rebuilding of each gate in order, starting at the northeast corner and moving counter-clockwise, describing each gate by name. As with everything in God's Word, careful inspection of seemingly insignificant details—like the names of Jerusalem's ancient gates—yields a treasure trove of insight. Seen through spiritual eyes, the gates of Jerusalem present a picture of the progressive development of a believer and of the church as a whole. The gates serve to remind us of how we are to live our Christian lives.

In God's fascinating spiritual picture in Nehemiah 3, the city represents the church, and the walls represent the separation between the church (i.e. all believers) and the world. *The wall does not represent divisions that separate Christians from Christians.* All Christians are included in the "city." Only those who could prove that they were truly Jews had the right to work on the wall's construction, and only those who are truly born-again believers, children of God, live in Christ and belong to his church. The gates are useful for entering and leaving, and they show that we are *in* the world even though we are not *of* it (John 17:16). We must not isolate ourselves from the world; rather, we should *use* the "gates" as we grow and mature as believers.

What is the significance of the number of ancient Jerusalem's gates? Some see that, in the Bible, the number *ten* pictures responsibility. There were Ten Commandments on the two stone tablets, showing man's responsibility and duty toward God and his fellow man. The Jews were responsible to support the priests and Levites and the worship of God in the temple, and their gifts and offerings were counted in increments of 10% (tithes). The ten virgins in the parable the Lord Jesus taught in Matthew chapter 25 were responsible to keep their lamps trimmed in anticipation of the bridegroom's arrival.

We will find responsibilities—Christian duties—that correspond to each of the ten gates. They also speak of our responsibility to be separated from the world. The gates were opened and closed at specified times, and we, likewise, have both the responsibility and the privilege of using their spiritual counterparts as we live out our lives each day. Again, this is not a question of leaving a particular church fellowship to find a place that suits us better; rather, it relates to our daily commerce and contact with the world. Remember the Lord's own personal petition to his Father: "My prayer is not that you take them out of the world but that you protect them from the evil one" (John 17:15).

Surviving (and even Thriving) in a Hostile Environment

The submarine provides a ready illustration for describing the truth that we are to be in the world but not of it. Water is not the natural habitat of human beings; we were not made to live under water—only fish and other aquatic creatures were. But when someone gets onboard a submarine, he can survive underwater because he has taken *his* environment—the air—with him. He is safe as long as he remains inside the submarine. If there is a hole in the submarine's outer structure, he is in great danger until the hole is repaired.

Christians are also in a foreign environment. We have become citizens of heaven, though we still live in a place where the "prince of this world" wants to smother us and take control of our lives

(Philippians 3:20; 1 Peter 5:8-9). Christ is our submarine. Because we are in Christ, we can safely live in the world, even though we are now aliens in relation to it. If a believer lets the world come into his life, he is like a submarine with a hole in it; he is in great danger—not of losing his salvation (because eternal life cannot be lost) but of regressing spiritually. We must, therefore, walk by the Spirit and not "gratify the desires of the flesh" (Galatians 5:16, RSV).

Exploring Jerusalem's gates will help us to see how we can find the holes in the hull—those areas where the flesh rules—and patch and prevent them while we serve the Lord in the world. Although it can be easy to forget that we are visitors ill-suited to our environment, a constant consciousness of that fact will help us maintain close fellowship with the Lord.

As we examine what each gate represents and begin to apply these principles to our lives, we will mature into Christ's likeness and live more effectively for him.

THE SHEEP GATE

Nehemiah 3:1~2

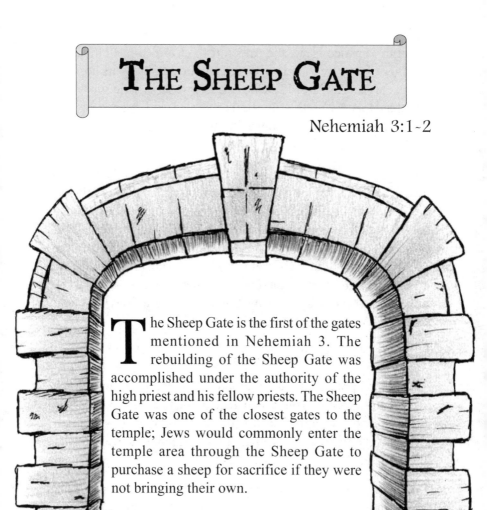

The Sheep Gate is the first of the gates mentioned in Nehemiah 3. The rebuilding of the Sheep Gate was accomplished under the authority of the high priest and his fellow priests. The Sheep Gate was one of the closest gates to the temple; Jews would commonly enter the temple area through the Sheep Gate to purchase a sheep for sacrifice if they were not bringing their own.

The Lamb—God's Prescribed Substitute

In order to approach God, the Jews had to first make a sacrifice for their sins as prescribed by the Law. Rams and lambs were the animals most often associated with such offerings. As Abraham walked up Mount Moriah with his son Isaac, he told him, "God himself will provide the lamb for the burnt offering." As Abraham was about to sacrifice Isaac, the Angel of the Lord stopped his hand and there, close by, Abraham noticed a ram caught by its horns in a thicket (Genesis 22:8, 13). God had required a sacrifice on which Abraham placed great value—his beloved son, Isaac, the one through who God had promised he would create a nation. Then God provided a *substitute* for Isaac.

We read in Exodus 12 that, at the climax of Moses' demands to Pharaoh that he free the children of Israel from bondage in Egypt, the angel of death passed over the land. It was only those households who had sprinkled the blood of an unblemished, sacrificed lamb on their doorposts and lintel that were spared the death of their firstborn child. This "lamb as substitute" principle was in force throughout the Old Testament until the Lord Jesus fulfilled the type. He was manifested as the "Lamb of God who takes away the sin of the world" (John 1:29).

Jesus Christ—the Lamb of God

Just as the application of the blood of the lamb began Israel's journey to freedom, so our acceptance of the Lamb's blood begins our journey to freedom; thus the Spirit of God moved Nehemiah to begin his record of the repair of Jerusalem's gates with the Sheep Gate.

The Christian life begins when a person recognizes the Lord Jesus as the Lamb whom God provided to give his life as our substitute. He was the perfect Lamb "without spot or blemish." On the basis of his sacrifice, God accepts all who acknowledge they are sinners and who place their faith in Christ.

> Yet to all who received him, to those who believed in his name, he gave the right to become children of God— children born not of natural descent, nor of human decision or a husband's will, but born of God (John 1:12-13).

God judged Christ for our sins. His death on the cross paid for them. We receive salvation and new life and we become members of Christ's body, the church, when we personally confess that

Christ died in our place. There is no other way to be saved. There is no other way to receive eternal life or enter into the abundant life the Lord offers.

In John 10:9-10 the Lord Jesus said, "I am the gate; whoever enters through me will be saved. He will come in and go out, and find pasture. . . . I have come that they

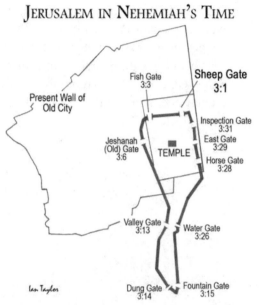

JERUSALEM IN NEHEMIAH'S TIME

Present Wall of Old City

Fish Gate 3:3

Sheep Gate 3:1

Inspection Gate 3:31

Jeshanah (Old) Gate 3:6

TEMPLE

East Gate 3:29

Horse Gate 3:28

Valley Gate 3:13

Water Gate 3:26

Ian Taylor

Dung Gate 3:14

Fountain Gate 3:15

may have life, and have it to the full." Just as only those priests who could prove their family line (genealogy) back to Aaron (the first high priest) were allowed to participate in temple life and service (Nehemiah 7:5, 61, 64), so only those who are "certified" or sealed by the permanently-indwelling Holy Spirit can enter into the enriching life that Christ provides for his own (Ephesians 1:13; Romans 8:9).

No Substitutions for God's Ordained Substitute

Some think they can enter into salvation through other gates, like the gate of good works or the gate of religion. Some even think they can buy their entry through the gate of donations to the church. But the Sheep Gate tells us that salvation is found only in Jesus Christ, the Lamb of God.

The Lord Jesus was near the Sheep Gate when he healed the paralyzed man at the pool of Bethesda (John 5:2). Although the Scripture is silent as to whether the man subsequently became a follower of the Lord Jesus, his miraculous capacity to walk again and the dramatic change that his healing must have meant to his life pictures the new life we enter into when we meet the Lord. *We* were once paralyzed with sin, with no one to help us. Jesus challenges us to acknowledge that we "want to get well" (John 5:6). He heals us—immediately and permanently. Thank God for the Sheep Gate, now the symbol for us of the place where we had a personal encounter with the One who enabled us to walk in newness of life.

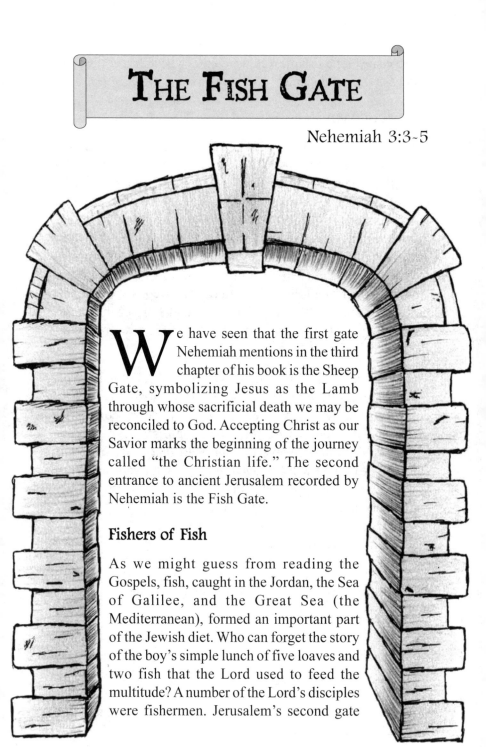

THE FISH GATE

Nehemiah 3:3-5

We have seen that the first gate Nehemiah mentions in the third chapter of his book is the Sheep Gate, symbolizing Jesus as the Lamb through whose sacrificial death we may be reconciled to God. Accepting Christ as our Savior marks the beginning of the journey called "the Christian life." The second entrance to ancient Jerusalem recorded by Nehemiah is the Fish Gate.

Fishers of Fish

As we might guess from reading the Gospels, fish, caught in the Jordan, the Sea of Galilee, and the Great Sea (the Mediterranean), formed an important part of the Jewish diet. Who can forget the story of the boy's simple lunch of five loaves and two fish that the Lord used to feed the multitude? A number of the Lord's disciples were fishermen. Jerusalem's second gate was the site of the fish market, which was where the people could purchase this food staple.

Fishers of Men

What spiritual significance is there to fish, and why should this gate follow the Sheep Gate? The Lord gives us a key to what fish and fishing represent when he calls Simon and Andrew to be his disciples. In Mark's gospel (the account that focuses most on the works of the Lord as obedient Servant) we read that Jesus said, "Come, follow me, and I will make you fishers of men" (Mark 1:16-17). The Fish Gate represents a new convert's turn *away* from self and *toward* selfless witness of Jesus Christ. Simon and Andrew would later follow in the Lord's footsteps and eventually be counted among those who laid the foundation for the church through their testimonies of what it was like to know and follow the Son of God.

The Lord wants all of his followers to be "fishers of men" from the beginning of their Christian lives. The Christian's outward confession that Jesus is his Lord is a necessary early component of the believer's spiritual growth. "If you confess with your mouth, 'Jesus is Lord,' and believe in your heart that God raised him from the dead, you will be saved. For it is with your heart that you believe and are justified, and it is with your mouth that you confess and are saved" (Romans 10:9-10).

Fish Bait: the Gospel

This confession with the mouth is not just a ritual to be checked off a list; it is part of the Lord's marvelous plan for the propagation of the gospel:

> How, then, can they call on the one they have not believed in? And how can they believe in the one of whom they have not heard? And how can they hear without someone preaching to them? And how can they preach unless they are sent? As it is written, 'How beautiful are the feet of those who bring good news!' (Romans 10:14-15)

This "good news" is the gospel. The apostle Paul did not wait even a single day to preach Christ after his sight was restored: "At once he began to preach in the synagogues that Jesus is the Son of God" (Acts 9:20). The early believers spoke out in the threat of persecution, as we also read in Acts: "Those who had been scattered preached [conversed] the word wherever they went" (Acts 8:4). They had an urgent desire to evangelize.

Jesus Said, "Go Fish!"

Whether or not we have been graced with the gift of evangelism, we should all be occupied with the work of winning the lost, and we should begin to do this work immediately after we are saved. Christ's commands to the disciples at that time are also commands for us today. "Therefore go and make disciples of all nations" (Matthew 28:19). "You will be my witnesses in Jerusalem, and in all Judea and Samaria, and to the ends of the earth" (Acts 1:8). These words have not lost any power, value, or importance, even though over two thousand years have passed since they were first uttered.

The Christian who does not use the Fish Gate will be lacking in an essential Christian experience. All of Jerusalem's gates were meant to be *used*; they were not just for show, or décor. Similarly, each gate's spiritual counterpart is meant to be used. Not only should individual believers be telling others of the Lord Jesus, but the local church should be as well. The local church

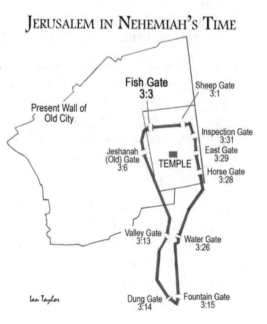

JERUSALEM IN NEHEMIAH'S TIME

Present Wall of Old City

Fish Gate
3:3

Sheep Gate
3:1

Inspection Gate
3:31

Jeshanah (Old) Gate
3:6

TEMPLE

East Gate
3:29

Horse Gate
3:28

Valley Gate
3:13

Water Gate
3:26

Ian Taylor

Dung Gate
3:14

Fountain Gate
3:15

should involve itself with some sort of gospel outreach, whether it is Sunday school, club work, camps, Bible studies, neighborhood visitations, or special events. The local church and individual believers should be involved in evangelism so that all may experience the joy of seeing others come through the Sheep Gate and be saved (Acts 2:47).

Some Excuses of Those Who Don't

Some might say, "Evangelism is not my gift," or "I'm not capable of evangelizing." But an honest self-examination would reveal these to be merely excuses. The Lord commands us to testify, and he has promised us power to do so (Acts 1:8). When he sent the Holy Spirit on the Day of Pentecost, the Spirit entered all the believers and they declared the wonders of God (Acts 2:11).

Romans 8:9 tells us that the same Holy Spirit is abiding in every true believer. If we are not willing to speak out about our salvation and tell of God's love and mercy; if we can express no gratitude about being forgiven of our sins; if we have no desire to testify about the eternal life that God offers; then we surely need to follow Paul's advice to the Corinthians: "Examine yourselves to see whether you are in the faith" (2 Corinthians 13:5).

The noblemen of Tekoa (Nehemiah 3:5) were unwilling to put their shoulders to the reconstruction work they were allotted. The work of building the wall was not only for their protection; it was also the work of the Lord. Maybe they felt a little too important to be doing manual labor like lifting stones or mixing cement, of working alongside the "blue collar" citizens. Perhaps their problem was pride.

If you find yourself mumbling excuses rather than speaking out for the Lord, ask yourself if pride is your problem. Are you ashamed to be connected with the One who took such a lowly position? Is pride the reason you do not want to proclaim the virtues of the One who died for you?

Some Blessings for Those Who Do

Thank God that the other men and women on Nehemiah's list *did* do their part, and for that they received the blessing of an "honorable mention" in the Word of God. Paul was able to say, "I am not ashamed of the gospel because it is the power of God for the salvation of everyone who believes" (Romans 1:16). Likewise, it has been assigned to us to share the gospel with others. There is no greater joy than leading a soul to Christ. It is a privilege to be a link in the chain of circumstances that the Lord uses to bring a sinner to repentance and salvation.

The apostle Paul rejoiced when he wrote to the Thessalonians saying, "For what is our hope, our joy, or the crown in which we will glory in the presence of our Lord Jesus when he comes? Is it not you?" (1 Thessalonians 2:19). Apart from the joy we experience in this life when we lead souls to the Lord, there will also be the joy of seeing in heaven these converts who will be our special prize and crown.

Maybe you feel comfortable that you *are* doing your part to share the gospel. Before you check the Fish Gate off the list, however, remember that the gospel we preach is not limited to what we *speak*. Our behavior should conform to our words:

> You yourselves are our letter, written on our hearts, known and read by everybody. You show that you are a letter from Christ, the result of our ministry, written not with ink but with the Spirit of the living God, not on tablets of stone but on tablets of human hearts (2 Corinthians 3:2-3).

Our lives are constantly preaching some message, good or bad. Let's make sure that our lives speak the same message as our words (see Philippians 1:27).

Think carefully about it. Are you using the Fish Gate? The second gate that speaks of the Christian life is an important work. "He who wins souls is wise" (Proverbs 11:30).

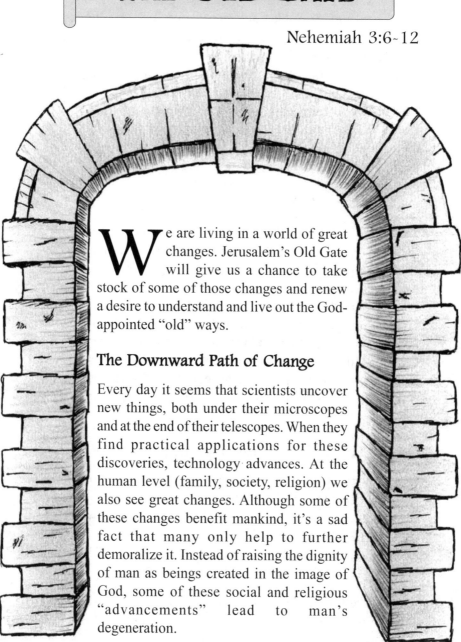

THE OLD GATE

Nehemiah 3:6-12

We are living in a world of great changes. Jerusalem's Old Gate will give us a chance to take stock of some of those changes and renew a desire to understand and live out the God-appointed "old" ways.

The Downward Path of Change

Every day it seems that scientists uncover new things, both under their microscopes and at the end of their telescopes. When they find practical applications for these discoveries, technology advances. At the human level (family, society, religion) we also see great changes. Although some of these changes benefit mankind, it's a sad fact that many only help to further demoralize it. Instead of raising the dignity of man as beings created in the image of God, some of these social and religious "advancements" lead to man's degeneration.

Modern thinkers in religious circles today are attacking the very foundations of the faith. The account of creation in Genesis is denied; some are working to erode basic doctrines and discredit entire books of the Bible; the inerrancy of Scripture is rejected; some view the virgin birth as a myth; the deity of Christ is argued; and the celebration of the Lord's Supper is either conducted as a mysterious rite or shuffled off to an occasional and relatively unimportant ceremony. We are losing the fear of God. Some Bible teachers are teaching from an imbalanced perspective that brings God down to man's level, treating him more like a buddy than the Almighty God. Because of this wrong attitude toward God, many churches have become more like social clubs than what they were intended to be—powerhouses, in which a holy and mighty God transforms lives.

The Old Gate teaches us to learn about and stay on the old paths. We must repair what has been damaged in the church and society at large, especially our beliefs concerning gender roles. But we have much other Old Gate repair work to do. Much Bible teaching is being diluted and shifting morals are infecting the Lord's work, resulting in a mire of rotten doctrines and a growing number of lukewarm, weak, and carnal Christians who are not very useful for the Lord's work. "This is what the LORD says: 'Stand at the crossroads and look; ask for the ancient paths, ask where the good way is, and walk in it, and you will find rest for your souls'" (Jeremiah 6:16).

Gender Roles: Biblical Teaching under Attack

One of the most significant ways in which this degradation of the faith has become apparent is the modern-day roles of men and women in the church. Confusion over these roles is wreaking havoc in the church and society at large. The subject of gender roles is such an important one that, for a moment, this discussion of the ancient and new paths will focus on this topic.

Although Scripture clearly defines men and women's roles in the church, some people seek to reverse these teachings. It is tragic that many among the unbelieving masses see Christians as confused buffoons in a laughable parody of the Truth. It is time for men and women to wholeheartedly fulfill their roles and get back to the basics of Scripture, taking the church to a higher level of credibility in the world's eyes.

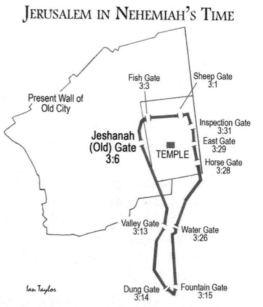

JERUSALEM IN NEHEMIAH'S TIME

The Man's Role

Men are not fulfilling their role in the family and local churches in many ways. Men, answer the following questions to help you assess whether you are living up to the work assigned to you.

1. Is church a "Sunday thing" or is church life, with its related activities, an integral part of your life? Are you a participating member of your local church or are you more of a "bench warmer"? Are you using your God-given spiritual gifts and abilities to help build up the local church?

2. Are you taking the lead in the spiritual welfare of your family?

3. Do you love your wife as Christ loves the church and as much as you love your own body (Ephesians 5:25, 28)?

4. Do you respect your wife and look for opportunities to nurture and help her? (Remember that not being respectful of your wife will hinder your prayers—1 Peter 3:7.)

5. Can you honestly say that you are setting an example for your children to follow as you study the Word for yourself,

provide your children with spiritual guidance, and lead the family in devotion to God (Deuteronomy 6:6-9)?

Sadly, we men often fall short of what God expects of us when it comes to being actively involved in church ministries. The Word clearly teaches that men are to use their spiritual gifts to edify the church:

> It was he who gave some to be apostles, some to be prophets, some to be evangelists, and some to be pastors and teachers, to prepare God's people for works of service, so that the body of Christ may be built up. . . . From him the whole body, joined and *held together by every supporting ligament, grows and builds itself up in love, as each part does its work* (Ephesians 4:11-12, 16, italics added).

The exhortation is clear, but we often see men sitting back, taking it easy, and leaving the work to others. This often forces women to take up the slack. Men need to be the spiritual leaders God wants them to be, in the home and also in the local churches.

The Woman's Role

Just as men must be sure to stay on the "ancient path" of leadership, women should continue on the paths appointed to them. The lists of names in Nehemiah might seem boring at first glance, but such biblical lists are gems for the inquisitive Bible student. The careful reader will notice the brief mention of Shallum's daughters, who helped build the section of the wall near the Old Gate. We do not know if Shallum had any sons to help him, but whether he did or not, this was not an obstacle, for his daughters stepped forward and did their part. How precious is the Word of God! Though men are to be in authority over women, and women are not to preach (1 Timothy 2:11-12; 1 Corinthians 14:34-35), the woman's role on the ancient paths is absolutely vital. The sisters need to find the God-appointed ways specific to them as they equip themselves to walk in righteousness before the Lord.

In reality, men and women's respective works are intertwined. Although it is the men who should be "out in front" usually, women can help in every spiritual work with their presence, their prayers, their work, and their teaching at the appropriate times and places. As genders roles are attacked today, women also need to dig into the Word to separate truth from lies.

In the New Testament, references to the woman's role in the home and the church take no account of the customs of those days or culture. When answering a question about divorce, the Lord Jesus went back to a point before culture, to the Garden of Eden (Matthew 19:4-6). He spoke of the woman being subject to her husband and focused less on hierarchy and more on unity. When God joined our first parents, he said, "The two will become one flesh" (Genesis 2:24). It is not a matter of superiority (Ephesians 5:31); they are one unit with different functions. Any man seeking God's ancient paths will discover that his wife completes him such that he becomes capable of leading in a way he could not do without her. God's focus is on making a fully functioning "one" out of two separated halves who have need of each other.

Although God's focus is more on unity than hierarchy, man's leadership "assignment" is impossible to miss. Once again, the Holy Spirit (this time through the apostle Paul) goes back to the Garden of Eden to make this point. "I do not permit a woman to teach or to have authority over a man; she must be silent. For Adam was formed first, then Eve. And Adam was not the one deceived; it was the woman who was deceived and became a sinner" (1 Timothy 2:12-14). Because Eve was the first to be tempted and fail, God stated that the headship of the home would be the husband's role (Genesis 3:16b). Likewise, God would later confer leadership of the church upon men (1 Corinthians 14:33-34; 1 Timothy 2:11-14). God's reasoning concerning these roles goes back to creation, before culture began, thereby establishing norms for all generations and cultures.

Although Christian sisters are to be in submission to their husbands and are not to be the principal leaders in the churches, do not make the mistake of thinking that women are merely ornamental. On the contrary, the Word reveals much about the work assigned to them. Romans 16 records a list of many sisters who helped greatly in their churches, even collaborating with the work of the apostle Paul. We read in Titus 2:3-5 that the older women had the duty of teaching the younger ones to walk in the ancient paths. Yes, the sisters have an important part in the kingdom work as well as in repairing the damage done to these ancient paths.

Sexual Relationships: Another Biblical Teaching under Attack

It is vital that we work to repair degenerating concepts of gender roles. This work extends to the amazing degeneration of understanding concerning masculinity and femininity in general.

The "human rights" movement, like the feminist movement, started with good intentions: to gain appropriate justice for many who are suffering world-wide because of ignorance, political and religious oppression, the unequal distribution of commodities, and the never-ending assault of one nation against another. Once again, however, some who claim to be advocates of this movement have allowed their good intentions to become imbalanced. Those pushing the politically correct agenda want to remove others' rights to criticize homosexuality insisting, for example, that homosexuals be given the right to practice their immoral acts without censure. Businesses can no longer refuse to employ people simply because they are gay. Should we be forced to allow these who are, sadly, spiritual deviants, to teach our children? With gay churches, gay pastors, and even an openly homosexual bishop, just how far will this evil go? Let us put our shoulders to the work of restoring the ancient wall of appropriate sexual relationships.

A Biblical Example of a Return to the Old Paths

As we read the history of the kings of Israel we see that they often followed the practices of the nations around them, practicing idolatry and all the horrible immoral practices that went along with it, deserting the old paths established in the books of the Law. For that reason, God disciplined his people with the purpose of bringing them back to himself. Josiah was one of the kings who decided to follow the "old paths." He initiated the task of renovating and cleansing the temple. While doing this, a copy of the Law was discovered and when King Josiah read it, he realized just how far the nation had strayed from God. He began to put into practice the teachings of the Law (2 Kings 22:1-23:30). The actions of Josiah illustrate for us what the Old Gate means. We need to get back into the Word and practice the principles and doctrines that it teaches.

Although you might say that we don't practice idolatry today, we need to ask ourselves some questions: What am I prioritizing ahead of the Lord? What activities or diversions are taking me away from a life of holiness, purity, or participation in the local church? Your answer may be the idol which you need to reject so that you can find God's will for your life and live for Him. Keeping Romans 12:1-2 in mind will help us keep our priorities and perspectives in proper focus: "Therefore, I urge you, brothers, in view of God's mercy, to offer your bodies as living sacrifices, holy and pleasing to God—this is your spiritual act of worship. Do not conform any longer to the pattern of this world, but be transformed by the renewing of your mind. Then you will be able to test and approve what God's will is—his good, pleasing and perfect will."

There Is Work for Everyone at the Old Gate

We have applied the work on the Old Gate to the need to return to the biblical standards of moral, ethical, and doctrinal practice. Nehemiah goes further, however, to show us that diligently learning the old ways and keeping them in good repair is work for everyone, rich and poor, white-collar and blue-collar, regardless of our situations and talents. In chapter 3 verses 6-12, we see a surprising list of people with many different occupations and status levels who set about reconstructing the Old Gate and its surrounding walls. No one was excluded.

Uzziel was a goldsmith, accustomed to delicate work with precious metals. He was probably a wealthy man of high social status, but he put this position aside in order to carry rough stones and heavy rocks. It is likely that he was not accustomed to such work, but it was necessary work for his own safety and that of the entire community—the work of securing the future. He had to put aside his profitable business for a while, sacrificing material gain in pursuit of that security. By doing so, he achieved a more enduring and more valuable work, one that is recorded eternally in God's Word. All of us who labor for the Lord according to his instructions and who follow the ancient paths are participating in a fine work, the results of which are like precious metals stored away for all eternity (1 Corinthians 3:12-15).

Following Uzziel the goldsmith we find another who had an intellectual profession, a job that probably didn't require much physical exertion. It's hard to imagine a job more different from heavy construction that Hananiah's usual work, that of perfume making. A perfumer of the time would have spent years learning about medicinal herbs and remedies. He would have applied this learning to his studies of the fragrant plants and chemicals needed to produce perfumes and medicinal spices. Perfume-makers were akin to doctors in those days. Uzziel would have been accustomed to working in his shop, mixing powders and drying plants—not working in the out-of-doors mixing cement!

Even the perfume-maker, however, had to do his part to repair the portion of wall assigned to him near the Old Gate. No doubt his hands became blistered and his back ached every night, but no one else could do the work for him. He may not have produced many perfumes while he worked on the wall, but he offered up his work on the wall as a pleasing fragrance to the Lord, and his example has been a sweet perfume of testimony for the millions who have since read the book of Nehemiah.

We also read about two of Jerusalem's rulers working on this section of the wall, Rephaiah and Shallum (whose daughters were mentioned earlier). As politicians and leaders, Rephaiah and

Shallum could have sent servants or paid others to do their part. But as true leaders of God's people, they led by example, not command. We need to see the same in the church today. The elders must teach and govern, ". . . not lording it over those entrusted to [them], but being examples to the flock" (1 Peter 5:3; see also 1 Timothy 5:17).

The rich, the poor, the intellectuals, the professionals, men and women—none were excluded from this work at the Old Gate.

Choosing and Using the Old Gate

The Jews living in Jerusalem had to put their shoulders to the work of repairing the Old Gate, and they had to learn how to work together to do it. Perhaps they took their lesson from the story of Isaac and his father's wells.

Isaac's father, Abraham, had dug several wells for water, but enemies had filled them in. In order for Isaac to be able to live in the land, he had to reopen these sources of life. "Isaac reopened the wells that had been dug in the time of his father Abraham, which the Philistines had stopped up after Abraham died, and he gave them the same names his father had given them" (Genesis 26:18). The wells were still good, and the old names were respected and kept, but Isaac had to do some work himself to make use of them. In the same way, the old pathways of the faith, established on the authority of the Word, are proven safe and lead to life.

In his surpassing wisdom, God placed the Old Gate after the Fish Gate. When Christians fulfill their duty to bring souls to the Lord and experience the joy of seeing them eternally secure in Christ, it is vital that they take the new convert to the local church where he or she will learn of the God-appointed ancient paths. False paths abound, and there are so many "wolves" prowling today that the new Christian needs a firm grounding in Scripture taught by those who can mentor them. We have a great need for more teaching about holiness and true discipleship today! Such teaching will help them become firmly established on the foundation of Scripture so that they will "no longer be infants, tossed back and forth by the waves, and blown here and there by every wind of teaching and by the cunning and craftiness of men in their deceitful scheming" (Ephesians 4:14).

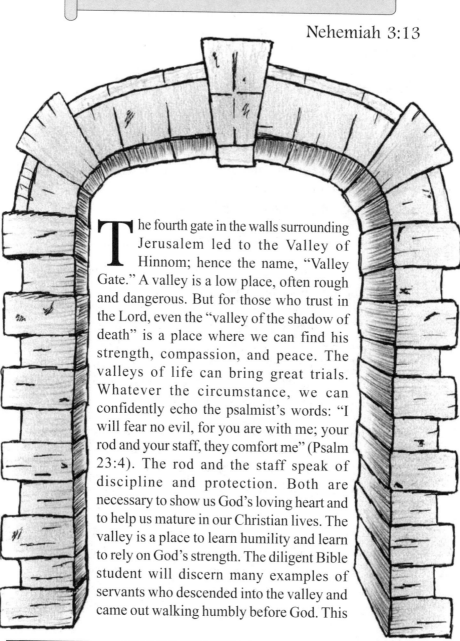

THE VALLEY GATE

Nehemiah 3:13

The fourth gate in the walls surrounding Jerusalem led to the Valley of Hinnom; hence the name, "Valley Gate." A valley is a low place, often rough and dangerous. But for those who trust in the Lord, even the "valley of the shadow of death" is a place where we can find his strength, compassion, and peace. The valleys of life can bring great trials. Whatever the circumstance, we can confidently echo the psalmist's words: "I will fear no evil, for you are with me; your rod and your staff, they comfort me" (Psalm 23:4). The rod and the staff speak of discipline and protection. Both are necessary to show us God's loving heart and to help us mature in our Christian lives. The valley is a place to learn humility and learn to rely on God's strength. The diligent Bible student will discern many examples of servants who descended into the valley and came out walking humbly before God. This humility and dependence on the Father formed the basis upon which he was able to use them. These useful servants had personal encounters with God in which he revealed to them much about the sorry condition of their hearts, resulting in true humility. We will learn the importance of true humility through a study of the Valley Gate.

Humility: the Opposite of Pride

We gain clues to the nature of humility by looking at, and finding in ourselves, humility's opposite: pride. By nature, man tends to have a high estimation of himself, a vaunted view of his ideas and abilities. Those who are "blessed" with many possessions are often prone to be proud. Possessions often carry power and influence, neither of which promotes humility. The Lord warned Israel to beware of this kind of material gain because he knew that it would lead to spiritual and moral degeneration:

> Be careful that you do not forget the Lord your God, failing to observe his commands, his laws and his decrees that I am giving you this day. Otherwise, when you eat and are satisfied, when you build fine houses and settle down, and when your herds and flocks grow large and your silver and gold increase and all you have is multiplied, then your heart will become proud and you will forget the Lord your God (Deuteronomy 8:11-14).

Unregenerate man seeks to be totally independent, to be self-sufficient, to control his own destiny. This is pride. The opposite of humility is a kind of self-worship (idolatry) that says, "I am the master of my fate. I am responsible for my situation, good or bad."

True humility places God alone on the throne as the omnipotent and eternal Master of the universe, the controller of all situations, good and bad. How do we take ourselves off that throne and put God on it? If we want to understand what it means to be truly humble, we must first recognize that we have by nature a proud and deceitful heart. To see ourselves this way, we must come close to God's purity. In the presence of the Holy One we quickly understand our frailty, our smallness, our lack of wisdom, and our *impurity*. We see that, in our weakness, we control precious little. In our impurity, we are selfish and destructive. As we become conscious of God's greatness and power, we are able to get a clearer perspective of ourselves. Several Bible characters experienced this type of personal encounter with God, and the results in their lives were dramatic to say the least! Let's consider some of them.

Humility: the Response of Men Who Met God

Abraham, after speaking with God, said, "Now that I have been so bold as to speak to the Lord, though I am nothing but dust and ashes . . ." (Genesis 18:27). God created man from the dust of the earth. Abraham was seeing himself as nothing more than clay in the Creator's hands. This was an insightful self-evaluation.

Job justified himself to his accusing "comforters" who were trying to prove that his suffering was the result of sin in his life. In the process, Job spoke quite well of himself as a "righteous man." Then he encountered the truly righteous and holy One. At that time, Job sensed his real condition and didn't hesitate to say, "I am unworthy— how can I reply to you? I put my hand over my mouth" (Job 40:4). Later in his story, Job said, "My ears had heard of you

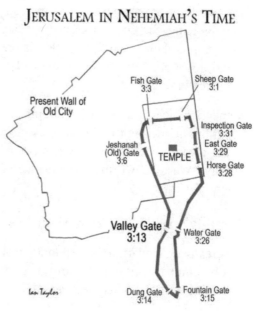

JERUSALEM IN NEHEMIAH'S TIME

Fish Gate 3:3

Sheep Gate 3:1

Present Wall of Old City

Inspection Gate 3:31

Jeshanah (Old) Gate 3:6

TEMPLE

East Gate 3:29

Horse Gate 3:28

Valley Gate 3:13

Water Gate 3:26

Ian Taylor

Dung Gate 3:14

Fountain Gate 3:15

but now my eyes have seen you. Therefore I despise myself and repent in dust and ashes" (Job 42:4-6). Job's humility was a prerequisite for all the blessings God had planned for him (Job 42:12-17).

David could say, after repenting and confessing his sin to God, "The sacrifices of God are a broken spirit; a broken and contrite heart, O God, you will not despise" (Psalm 51:17). When we are willing to humble ourselves before God, confess our sin, and put away dependence on the flesh, we are in a position to be of greatest use to the Lord.

In Isaiah 5, the prophet denounced the sin of the nation, often beginning his accusations with "Woe to those . . ." (vv. 8, 11, 18, 20-22). What he said was true; it was the word of the Lord. But it is interesting to observe his reaction when he himself entered God's holy presence. In chapter 6, reacting to the vision of the Lord and seeing the seraphim (angels) who were saying, "Holy, holy, holy is the Lord Almighty; the whole earth is full of his glory," he did not look *outward* to say, "Woe to those . . ." but instead said, "Woe to me! I am ruined! For I am a man of unclean lips, and I live among a people of unclean lips, and my eyes have seen the King, the Lord Almighty" (v. 5). A seraph then touched his mouth and cleansed him so that later, when God asked who would go to proclaim his message to Israel, Isaiah was able to say, "Here am I. Send me!" (v. 8).

We need to have this kind of encounter with the Lord in order to stop thinking too highly of ourselves. As the Lord does his work in and through us, he alone will receive the glory, because we will say, "We are unworthy servants; we have only done our duty" (Luke 17:10).

Humility's Fruit: Self-denial and Service to Others

After realizing God's utter sovereignty in our lives and his holiness (and by comparison, our lack of power and impurity), we must trust that he will give us the strength to practice self-denial: "If anyone would come after me, he must deny himself and take up his cross daily and follow me" (Luke 9:23). The apostle Paul gave Christ as our example here:

> Do nothing out of selfish ambition or vain conceit, but in humility consider others better than yourselves. Each of you should look not only to your own interests, but also to the interests of others. Your attitude should be the same as that of Christ Jesus . . . he humbled himself (Philippians 2:3-8).

We must not trust in our strength, intelligence, or abilities. We have to recognize that "nothing good lives in me, that is, in my sinful nature" (Romans 7:18). We must let him, the Creator of all things, take this clay to mold it according to his purposes, so that it can become a useful vessel, ready and willing for every work he gives us. Paul understood that his spiritual strength did not come from himself. When he felt the least confident in his own strength, he was stronger, because his trust was completely in the Lord. The resulting strength was the demonstration of the Almighty in a vessel of clay: "For when I am weak, then I am strong" (2 Corinthians 12:10).

Be Humble about Humility

A word of caution: after understanding what true humility is and experiencing some of God's power in our lives, we are in danger of thinking that we have reached true spirituality and humility. We must beware of such attitudes and heed well the warning: "If you think you are standing firm, be careful that you don't fall!" (1 Corinthians 10:12). When we think we have attained true humility, we need to immediately come close to the Lord, because pride is starting to raise its ugly head. Unless this attitude is corrected, we will soon fall.

A truly humble person does not think of himself; he thinks of others. Our love and patience towards our brethren will manifest our humility. How am I serving my fellow believers? Am I willing to let others take advantage of me? What is my response when they mistreat me? The brother who demonstrates true humility will never be the cause of division or conflict among God's people. The humble brother will put others before himself:

> Therefore, as God's chosen people, holy and dearly loved, clothe yourselves with compassion, kindness, humility, gentleness and patience. Bear with each other and forgive whatever grievances you may have against one another. Forgive as the Lord forgave you (Colossians 3:12-13).

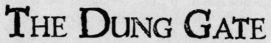

THE DUNG GATE

Nehemiah 3:14

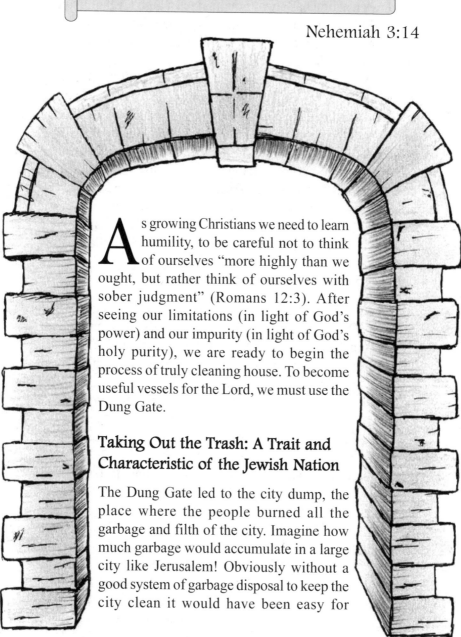

As growing Christians we need to learn humility, to be careful not to think of ourselves "more highly than we ought, but rather think of ourselves with sober judgment" (Romans 12:3). After seeing our limitations (in light of God's power) and our impurity (in light of God's holy purity), we are ready to begin the process of truly cleaning house. To become useful vessels for the Lord, we must use the Dung Gate.

Taking Out the Trash: A Trait and Characteristic of the Jewish Nation

The Dung Gate led to the city dump, the place where the people burned all the garbage and filth of the city. Imagine how much garbage would accumulate in a large city like Jerusalem! Obviously without a good system of garbage disposal to keep the city clean it would have been easy for contagious diseases to spread. Cleanliness was necessary for the well-being of the individual as well as the community as a whole.

The Jewish nation has always maintained a high level of hygiene (derived from standards set in the Law God gave to Moses) and, historically, this practice has protected the Jews from many of the plagues that have decimated other people groups. During the Middle Ages, many Europeans did not understand the necessity for proper hygiene. Garbage was dumped indiscriminately and sewage was allowed to drain through city streets. This resulted in a proliferation of rats that carried the bubonic plague into many homes. As a result, untold thousands died. When people noticed that Jewish people, who lived together in ghettos, were not getting sick, they blamed them and persecuted them. The truth was that the Jews had such a good garbage disposal system and such a high level of personal hygiene that very few rats inhabited their neighborhoods. The plague, therefore, did not affect them.

The Need for Personal Spiritual Purity

Looking at the spiritual lessons of the Dung Gate we can see that it relates (1) to the personal purity and holiness of the individual believer, and (2) to the collective purity and cleanliness of the local church or assembly. We can readily see that both of these are necessary for the health of the whole. If there is even only one person who is not practicing spiritual "hygiene," that person can start a "plague" that can affect the whole local church. From the very first pages of Scripture we see that God places great emphasis on dealing with sin so that we can walk before Him in holiness. God covered Adam and Eve with the skins of animals (sacrificed for them) to hide their shame. Abel sacrificed an animal to cover his sins, and God accepted his sacrifice. Because King Saul did not truly repent from his sin, he lost his kingdom. King David sinned grievously and went through great anguish before he repented and confessed his sin. He knew that he had lost fellowship with God (Psalm 51:1-12). After Peter denied the Lord, he repented, was restored, and went on to preach the first message of the church at Pentecost, when thousands were saved.

When a Believer Sins

When a believer sins, he loses fellowship with God, the Father. To understand the reason for this, we must understand that God is perfectly holy. The seraphim around God's throne work to proclaim God's great holiness. Before the prophet Isaiah could speak or act for God, it was necessary for one of the seraphim to cleanse his lips with a burning coal. Isaiah

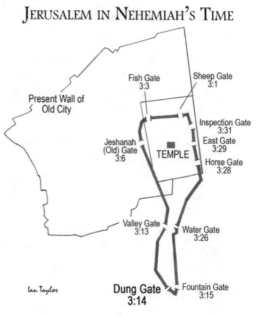

JERUSALEM IN NEHEMIAH'S TIME

Present Wall of Old City

Fish Gate 3:3

Sheep Gate 3:1

Inspection Gate 3:31

Jeshanah (Old) Gate 3:6

TEMPLE

East Gate 3:29

Horse Gate 3:28

Valley Gate 3:13

Water Gate 3:26

Ian Taylor

Dung Gate 3:14

Fountain Gate 3:15

felt his impurity in the presence of God. Before he was cleansed, his fellowship with God was hindered, squelched by fear and guilt (Isaiah 6:1-8). Isaiah's experience is common to man. When we sin, we inhibit the work of God's Spirit in us. Before exploring this topic further, let's establish some basics about the Holy Spirit.

When we accept the Lord Jesus as our Savior, the Spirit of God begins working in us. He gives us new life through regeneration (Titus 3:5) and seals us for the day of redemption (Ephesians 1:13; 4:30). The "day of redemption" does not refer to the day we were saved but to the day when Christ will return to redeem us from the earth and its corruption. The Holy Spirit also baptizes us into the body of Christ (1 Corinthians 12:13). He enters the believer to indwell him for the rest of his life here on earth (Romans 8:9; 1 Corinthians 6:19-20). The Spirit does all these things automatically at the moment of our conversion. We do not need to experience them either in the emotional or physical sense to know that they have happened; we believe that they have happened because the Bible says they have.

However, we also read in the Bible the command to "be filled with the Spirit" (Ephesians 5:18). Because this is a command, being filled with the Spirit is obviously not automatic; it is something we must seek and receive as we fulfill the divine requirements. The main point about the Spirit for this discussion, however, is that when we accept the Lord Jesus as our Savior and start our Christian life, the Spirit comes to dwell in us—in our bodies. Think about that! Paul wrote to the believers at Corinth:

> Do you not know that your body is a temple of the Holy Spirit, who is in you, whom you have received from God? You are not your own (1 Corinthians 6:19).

If the Holy Spirit lives in my body and I lend my body or mind to sin, this is an insult to God. It infringes on his holiness and results in loss of fellowship with him. Paul went on to reason with the Corinthians this way:

The body is not meant for sexual immorality, but for the Lord, and the Lord for the body. Do you not know that your bodies are members of Christ himself? Shall I then take the members of Christ and unite them with a prostitute? Never! But he who unites himself with the Lord is one with him in spirit (1 Corinthians 6:13-17).

When a Christian sins—whether by committing a sin that people consider serious or something we reckon to be insignificant, like an evil thought, jealousy, or a bad word—he offends the Holy Spirit dwelling in him. "And do not grieve the Holy Spirit of God, with whom you were sealed for the day of redemption" (Ephesians 4:30). If the Spirit is grieved because of unconfessed sin, we will not have his power or direction in our lives which, in turn, will lead to failure. We will look further at the work of the Holy Spirit in the next chapter, on the subject of the Fountain Gate.

In order to be in fellowship with the Lord and thus fit to be used by him, we must be clean, harboring no secret sins, because sin hinders the work of the Spirit in us and through us. "If a man cleanses himself . . . he will be an instrument for noble purposes, made holy, useful to the Master and prepared to do any good work" (2 Timothy 2:21).

God's Provision for the Sinning Saint

Though the consequences of sin for the believer are grave (discipline, broken fellowship, etc), the Bible clearly shows that when a believer sins he does not lose his salvation. The apostle John, in his first epistle, states that we *all* have sin in our lives, and if we say we do not, we make God out "to be a liar." But "if we confess our sins, he is faithful and just and will forgive us our sins and purify us from all unrighteousness" (1 John 1:8-10). John continues by saying that part of Christ's present work, as he sits at God's right hand, is to intercede for us as our advocate when we do sin (1 John 2:1). Although God commands us not to sin, he knows that we will, and he has graciously made provision for those times. When we sin, we have One to whom we must confess in order to receive forgiveness and cleansing.

God's Purpose for the Sanctified Saint

The apostle Paul set his Philippian readers (and us) the example of continuously and steadfastly aspiring to spiritual perfection and completion:

> I press on toward the goal to win the prize for which God has called me heavenward in Christ Jesus (Philippians 3:12-14).

We must honestly desire to "purify ourselves from everything that contaminates body and spirit, perfecting holiness out of reverence for God" (2 Corinthians 6:17-7:1).

We must confess all known sin and determine not to commit such a sin again. We should not try to excuse ourselves by saying that the temptation was too great to resist. We fall because we choose to continue thinking about it until it produces its fruit—sin: "But each one is tempted when, by his own evil desire, he is dragged away and enticed. Then, after desire has conceived, it gives birth to sin; and sin, when it is full-grown, gives birth to death" (James 1:14-15).

When temptation comes along we should look for the escape route, because God has promised a way to escape each situation: "No temptation has seized you except what is common to man. And God is faithful; he will not let you be tempted beyond what you can bear. But when you are tempted, he will also provide a way out so that you can stand up under it" (1 Corinthians 10:13). We cannot blame the devil, God, others, or our circumstances when we fail. When we look into our hearts, we see that we have cultivated sin long before we commit it. We must eliminate the cause: we must pull the roots out at their source, not just cut off some of the branches of the mature tree. Digging out and discarding these roots is represented by individual and personal use of the Dung Gate.

The Need for Corporate Spiritual Purity

The church at Corinth provides a good example of a church infected by lack of understanding concerning holiness and other doctrinal issues. In Paul's first epistle to the Corinthian church, the apostle reprimanded those who were dividing the church and lifting up men to take the place of Christ as the church's head (ch. 1). The Corinthians were not growing, because they were worldly (ch. 3). They did not know how to handle a case of gross immorality among their members (ch. 5). They were suing each other and not comprehending that practicing sex outside marriage, drunkenness, greed, and various kinds of injustices are all outside the norms of Christ's teachings (ch. 6). They were experiencing marital problems, and divorce was common (ch. 7). They were on the fringes of idolatry (ch. 10). They had turned the remembrance of the Lord into a drunken party (ch. 11). They grossly abused some of the gifts, and the meetings were generally disorderly (ch. 14). What did they have to do to clean up the local church? They needed to use the Dung Gate. They needed to deal with each case of sin by judging it and rejecting it.

Scriptural Forms of Discipline

Scripture provides various forms of discipline for the church to use to deal with different sin situations that involve an unrepentant sinning member. The appropriate form of discipline should be used with respect to the sin committed. Unfortunately, some churches simplify the act of discipline by either cutting off fellowship with the person too quickly or treating the issue so lightly that the person feels little discomfort continuing in their lifestyle. This latter extreme usually stems from fear of offending people. Apart from these two extremes, it is sometimes the case that a church fails to use the form of discipline most appropriate to the particular situation.

The individuals who comprise any community understand that collective action is necessary if someone breaks the community's rules and laws. Such laws are established for the well-being of its citizens or members. In the same way, a believer should be aware that he is part of a local church family, and as such there may be a need for the elders to correct or discipline that person for unchristian behavior. There are differing forms of discipline mentioned in the New Testament. These include:

- ✓ Admonishment (Romans 15:14; 1 Thessalonians 5:14; Titus 3:10)

- ✓ Isolation (2 Thessalonians 3:6, 14-15)

- ✓ Public Rebuke (Galatians 2:11-14; 1 Timothy 5:20)

- ✓ Silence (1 Peter 4:11; 1 Timothy 1:3-4; Titus 1:10-11)

- ✓ Excommunication (1 Corinthians 5:5-7, 13)

It is important that all believers recognize the need for accountability and submission to the Lord, to the Word, and to the elders in the local church. "Obey your leaders and submit to their authority. They keep watch over you as men who must give an account. Obey them so that their work will be a joy, not a burden, for that would be of no advantage to you" (Hebrews 13:17).

Restoration: An Intrinsic Part of Church Discipline

A church should never exercise discipline without first studying the means of helping the one in sin so that he can one day be restored. Restoration is just as important as applying the disciplines in the first place. Galatians 6:1 says, "Brothers, if someone is caught in a sin, you who are spiritual should restore him gently. But watch yourself, or you also may be tempted." Anyone can fall into sin, and it is only by the grace of God that we are where we are.

Discipline is not a weapon, but a treatment; it is a remedy for the part of the body that is sick and in need of healing. Even in the case of the immoral man in 1 Corinthians 5, Paul exhorted the believers to receive again, in love, the one who had offended (see 2 Corinthians 2:5-11). But care must be taken that the restored saint does not fall back into the same old problems. Leviticus 14 contains a rather lengthy list of instructions on how to restore the leper after he is healed.

The principle we can draw is one of restoration. These Scriptures outline the measures the priest had to take in order to return the person to a normal life in the camp. We can see that it was a lengthy process, but one of much value, because its purpose was for the good of the affected person and for the well-being of the whole congregation.

While it is not pleasant to have to deal with "garbage," the Dung Gate teaches us important lessons for both our individual lives and our local churches.

THE FOUNTAIN GATE

Nehemiah 3:15

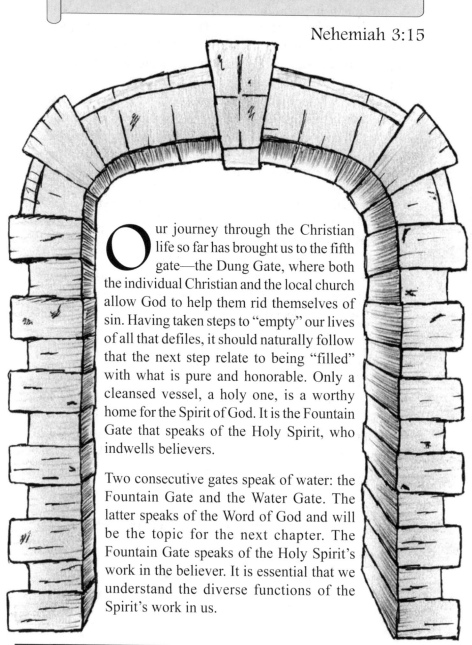

Our journey through the Christian life so far has brought us to the fifth gate—the Dung Gate, where both the individual Christian and the local church allow God to help them rid themselves of sin. Having taken steps to "empty" our lives of all that defiles, it should naturally follow that the next step relate to being "filled" with what is pure and honorable. Only a cleansed vessel, a holy one, is a worthy home for the Spirit of God. It is the Fountain Gate that speaks of the Holy Spirit, who indwells believers.

Two consecutive gates speak of water: the Fountain Gate and the Water Gate. The latter speaks of the Word of God and will be the topic for the next chapter. The Fountain Gate speaks of the Holy Spirit's work in the believer. It is essential that we understand the diverse functions of the Spirit's work in us.

Abundant Supply for Abundant Fruit

Regarding those who believe in him, the Lord Jesus promised that "streams of living water will flow from within him" (John 7:38). John adds in the next verse, "By this he meant the Spirit, whom those who believed in him were later to receive." Jesus did not just promise a puddle or a trickle; he promised "*streams of living water*." Streams, or rivers, usually originate from springs coming up out of the ground. They quench thirst and irrigate the land, making it fruitful. Rivers carry life to all who are within their reach. In applying the illustration of water to the work of the Holy Spirit in us, we discern the source of power that makes our lives a fertile field. The psalmist said:

> Blessed is the man who does not walk in the counsel of the wicked or stand in the way of sinners. . . . But his delight is in the law of the Lord, and on his law he meditates day and night. He is like a tree planted by *streams of water*, which yields its fruit in season and whose leaf does not wither. Whatever he does prospers (Psalm 1:1-4, italics added).

The righteous man is pictured as a tree whose life and fruit is sustained by a constant source of water. The strength every believer needs in order to flourish spiritually comes from the Spirit of God who indwells him, with the result that the believer produces abundant fruit for God's glory and honor. We, of ourselves, cannot produce spiritual fruit. We need the Holy Spirit to manifest His fruit in us, described as "love, joy, peace, patience, kindness, goodness, faithfulness, gentleness and self-control" (Galatians 5:22).

The Work of the Holy Spirit in Regeneration (Titus 3:5)

As we explore the vital role of the Spirit, we will start at the moment of spiritual birth. When children are born, they form the next generation for a family. *Generation* in this sense speaks of birth and new life; *regeneration* speaks of rebirth. The Lord Jesus spoke with Nicodemus about the need to be born again. He was not speaking about the natural birth of a baby into a family but about the spiritual birth that takes place when we are born into the family of God.

The Lord told him that he had to be born of water and of the Spirit (John 3:5). The water Christ spoke of in John 3:5 does not speak of baptism (as many contend) but of the Word of God. The Word is the two-edged sword that "penetrates even to dividing soul and spirit" (Hebrews 4:12). When a person hears the Word spoken or read, the Spirit convicts him of his sinful condition and his need for God's cleansing; God then produces faith in that person that enables him to believe and receive salvation. "Faith comes from hearing the message, and the message is heard through the word of Christ" (Romans 10:17). When a person hears the Word, the Spirit convicts. When the person responds to the message, the Spirit begins to reawaken the spiritual part of the person that was dead, the part that died in Adam in the Garden of Eden and lies dormant in each of Adam's descendants. When the Holy Spirit gives life, he does so automatically at the moment the person truly entrusts himself to the Lord Jesus Christ.

The Work of the Holy Spirit in Sealing (Ephesians 1:13; 4:3)

Seals are used to validate a document and to signify the official approval of the person who authorized it. In the days when Esther was queen, wicked

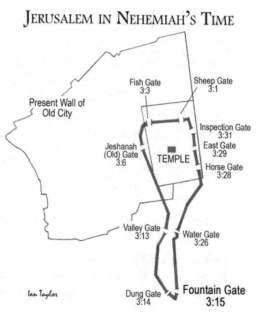

JERUSALEM IN NEHEMIAH'S TIME

Present Wall of Old City

Fish Gate 3:3

Sheep Gate 3:1

Inspection Gate 3:31

Jeshanah (Old) Gate 3:6

TEMPLE

East Gate 3:29

Horse Gate 3:28

Valley Gate 3:13

Water Gate 3:26

Ian Taylor

Dung Gate 3:14

Fountain Gate 3:15

Haman used the king's ring to seal the document ordering the annihilation of the Jews. Afterwards, Esther's Uncle Mordecai used the same ring to seal another decree in the king's name: the decree to save the Jews. In both cases, no one other than the king could revoke the decrees, because they had been sealed with the king's ring and were to be enforced by all (Esther 3:10-12; 8:8). This is the meaning of the sealing by the Holy Spirit. God has made a "contract" with believers. Because this contract is sealed with his own Spirit, it is legal and binding and cannot be revoked. The Spirit confirms the contract of salvation that is made on the basis of faith in Christ and his redemptive work at the cross. "He anointed us, set his seal of ownership on us, and put his Spirit in our hearts as a deposit, guaranteeing what is to come" (2 Corinthians 1:21-22).

The Spirit begins to live in believers in order to help us take possession of all the heavenly blessings that we have in Christ Jesus (Ephesians 1:3-12). He is our "deposit guaranteeing our inheritance until the redemption of those who are God's possession" (Ephesians 1:14). Note that we are sealed until "the day of redemption." These words are repeated in Ephesians 4:30. Paul is emphasizing that we can be certain of the eternal salvation of our souls. The Holy Spirit is given to every believer in order to confirm the contract made by God, and it will be in force until we enter into the fullness of our heavenly inheritance. What a wonderful promise! The Holy Spirit seals us automatically the moment we believe. It is not something that we can feel, nor do we have to work for it.

The Work of the Holy Spirit in Baptism
(Acts 1:5; 1 Corinthians 12:13-14)

The baptism of the Holy Spirit is a vital doctrine, second only to regeneration in importance. A cloud of confusion and misunderstanding surrounds this doctrine that has resulted in divisions in the body of Christ and discouragement among many. An interpretation of this doctrine nearer to truth should unite believers rather than divide them. Some teach either that the Spirit's baptism is a second blessing after salvation or that we need to beg him to come to us some time after being born again. Both ideas fall short of the truth and need to be rejected. Satan has sown this confusion, knowing the doctrine's importance.

Before exploring the Spirit's baptism further, we need to understand what the word "baptism" means. How is it used in the Bible and other ancient texts? *Baptism* is a transliteration (not a translation) of the Greek word *baptizo,* meaning to immerse or to sink. Ancient Greek writers used the word to describe the sinking of a ship and the invasion of a city where the conquering soldiers overran it. In the Septuagint (the Greek translation of the Old Testament) the translators used the word "baptize" for the word "wash" in Naaman's healing, when he dipped himself seven times in the Jordan. Another usage of the word was to dye a material by submerging it in a dye of a different color, as in "I *baptized* the material in red." The material lost its original color, becoming totally identified with the new color instead. These examples are enough to teach us that baptize means to submerge or immerse.

With these meanings in mind we have a better understanding of what is meant by the Spirit's baptism when we read: "For we were all baptized by one Spirit into one body" (1 Corinthians 12:13). It is the work of the Spirit to submerge us into the body of Christ so that we form part of one body made up of many different members. Spirit baptism is a work of overwhelming *disconnection* and *reconnection*, a severing of the old ties to the world and the forging of new connections to others who have, and will, accept Christ. This is what happened on the day of Pentecost when the Spirit descended to unite into one body all of Christ's followers. It was the fulfillment of the promise that the Lord gave them just before he ascended into heaven (Acts 1:5).

We must understand that the baptism of the Spirit is something that takes place at the moment of conversion and is not an experience subsequent to it. Acts 2 (the scene at Pentecost) does not even mention the baptism of the Spirit, because this aspect of the Spirit's work was (and is) not something that is seen or felt. In Acts 2 the disciples spoke in tongues and accomplished miraculous signs showing that they were *filled* with the Holy Spirit. This filling is a different work and should not be confused with the Spirit's baptism. The Holy Spirit's baptism is tremendously important because it is what he does to make us members of Christ's body and to identify us fully with the Lord Jesus and his people.

We often use Romans 6 to explain Christian water baptism. Water baptism is a step of obedience for the believer to show the world that he has died with Christ to the old life and now wants to live a new life in the power of the Spirit. It is permissible to use Romans 6 for this purpose, but we should understand that this chapter is really speaking, not of the water baptism that occurs *some time after conversion*, but of the Spirit's baptism *the moment we believe*. It is this baptism that empowers us to live our new life. Baptism by water is an outward sign of obedience that should follow the work that the Spirit has done in the new believer's heart. At the moment we believe, we are "immersed" into the body of Christ, identified with him in his death. With the new life given by the Spirit, he also gives us power to live it to the same degree with which Christ was raised from the dead (Ephesians 1:19-20).

Peter, in his first epistle, compared the Spirit's baptism to the rescue of Noah and his family, who were saved from God's judgment because they were inside the ark, secure and protected (1 Peter 3:21-22). The Holy Spirit places us in Christ, not only to function as members of his body but also to enjoy the only place where we find safety and security.

Understanding the doctrine of the Spirit's baptism should fill us with a desire to walk in a manner worthy of the Lord and to strive to keep the unity of the Spirit (Ephesians 4:1-5). If we are not conscious of being a part of Christ's body, united by the Spirit with all believers, we begin to malfunction in such a way that breeds contention, division, and an unhealthy individualism.

On the other hand, when we understand that we are "one in Christ," we will enjoy fellowship with other believers and be encouraged to serve one another (1 Corinthians 12:20-27). We will then begin to appreciate all the blessings we have as members of Christ's body, recognizing that each member has been placed there to function in coordination with all the other members under the guidance and leadership of the Head to whom we are all joined (Ephesians 1:22-23).

The Work of the Holy Spirit in Indwelling (Romans 8:9)

We have seen that the Holy Spirit performs several functions at the moment a person truly believes in Christ as his Savior. Generally we do not realize that these monumental changes are happening, nor do we understand these works even in theory at that time, because we are only babes in Christ. They happen automatically and do not depend on our understanding. All of these acts of the Spirit are included under the general term "indwelling" of the Spirit.

Several Bible passages make it clear that the Spirit dwells in all who are saved. The apostle Paul experienced a struggle in his life between his flesh and his spirit. There was conflict between the old man of sin and the new Spirit-given life that he enjoyed in Jesus Christ. He noticed that he, by himself, could not defeat the sinful desires of the flesh, nor did he have the power to live the Christian life as he ought: "What a wretched man I am! Who will rescue me from this body of death?" (Romans 7:24; read also verses 14-25).

Paul discovered the "secret" and wrote about it in Romans 8, where he describes the life lived by the Holy Spirit who gives power and direction to the believer. Paul exclaimed, "You, however, are controlled not by the sinful nature but by the Spirit, if the Spirit of God lives in you. And if anyone does not have the Spirit of Christ, he does not belong to Christ" (Romans 8:9). Paul establishes right away that the person who does not have the Spirit living in him is not Christ's—he is not saved.

Being Mindful of the Spirit's Indwelling

The Corinthians were ". . . worldly—mere infants in Christ" (1 Corinthians 3:1). Although they had grown spiritually in some ways, they had degenerated morally and in practical Christian living. We were reminded in the preceding chapter of the sad state of the Corinthian church: the lawsuits between believers, divisions, serious marital problems, and corruption of the Lord's Supper. This behavior was unworthy of the Lord (1 Corinthians 11:17-22). Yet Paul addressed his letter to them this way: "To those sanctified in Christ Jesus" (1 Corinthians 1:2)! They were truly saved, but he later reminded them of an important fact: "Don't you know that you yourselves are God's temple and that God's Spirit lives in you?" (1 Corinthians 3:16).

It is amazing that, in spite of their spiritual condition, the Spirit of God still indwelt them, both corporately and individually. This should be a cause for continual thanksgiving to God because, if his living in us depends on *our* condition, he would never be able to live in anyone! This is one of the reasons the doctrine of the indwelling Spirit is so important. We should always be conscious of his presence in us so that we do nothing to grieve him.

The study of the person and work of the Holy Spirit is extensive, and we have only been able to scratch the surface of it. The Fountain Gate, representing the power of the Spirit in the believer's life, is an important gate that we sometimes neglect. We should use it continually so that our lives will be productive. We should be conscious of the fact that the Holy Spirit is in us and—when he is given his way—he will lead us into fruitfulness and blessing.

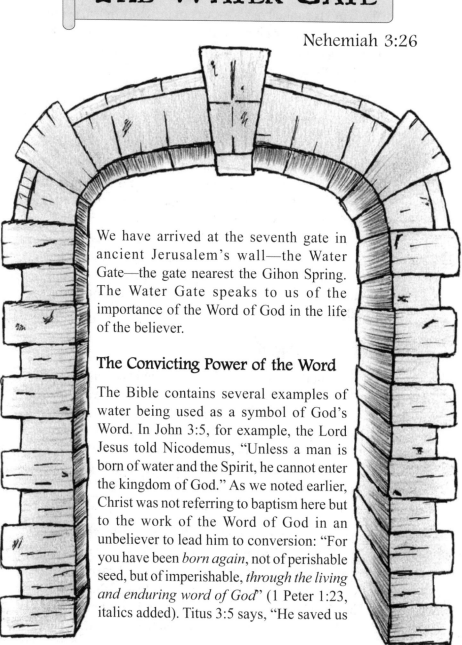

THE WATER GATE

Nehemiah 3:26

We have arrived at the seventh gate in ancient Jerusalem's wall—the Water Gate—the gate nearest the Gihon Spring. The Water Gate speaks to us of the importance of the Word of God in the life of the believer.

The Convicting Power of the Word

The Bible contains several examples of water being used as a symbol of God's Word. In John 3:5, for example, the Lord Jesus told Nicodemus, "Unless a man is born of water and the Spirit, he cannot enter the kingdom of God." As we noted earlier, Christ was not referring to baptism here but to the work of the Word of God in an unbeliever to lead him to conversion: "For you have been *born again*, not of perishable seed, but of imperishable, *through the living and enduring word of God*" (1 Peter 1:23, italics added). Titus 3:5 says, "He saved us through the *washing of rebirth and renewal by the Holy Spirit*" (italics added).

When the Word is applied by the power of the Holy Spirit, people are convicted "of sin, of righteousness and judgment" (John 16:8). We can be sure that, when the Word of God is presented, it *will* have an effect on the hearer.

> My word . . . will not return to me empty, but will accomplish what I desire and achieve the purpose for which I sent it (Isaiah 55:11).

God's Word has power and is destined to fulfill his purposes. One of these purposes is the evangelization and salvation of sinners. The phrase, "will not return to me empty," means that the Word of God will produce the desired fruit. The Word of God that is proclaimed through preaching, gospel tracts, radio programs, personal conversations with unbelievers, or any other method, will achieve its purpose. "Faith comes from hearing the message, and the message is heard through the word of Christ" (Romans 10:17).

The Cleansing Power of the Word

The Word does not only powerfully convict unbelievers; it is in continuous action in the lives of believers as well. The believer needs the daily application of the Word in his life to be continually cleansed. This is *progressive sanctification*, a growth process related to the believer's condition and not to his salvation position in Christ. The Lord Jesus gave himself for the church in order "to make her holy, cleansing her by *the washing with water through the word*" (Ephesians 5:26, italics added).

God has given us many pictures of how life in the flesh can corrupt us and of how we need to be continually cleansed. One such picture concerns the priests and the bronze laver in the tabernacle. The priests had to use the laver regularly to cleanse their hands and feet. They had been consecrated and were fit for the work of the Lord, but every day the priests had to remove all the dirt with which they had been contaminated through their contact with the dry earth.

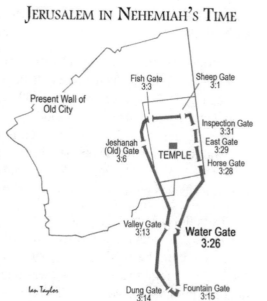

JERUSALEM IN NEHEMIAH'S TIME

Fish Gate 3:3
Sheep Gate 3:1
Present Wall of Old City
Inspection Gate 3:31
Jeshanah (Old) Gate 3:6
TEMPLE
East Gate 3:29
Horse Gate 3:28
Valley Gate 3:13
Water Gate 3:26
Ian Taylor
Dung Gate 3:14
Fountain Gate 3:15

The world is filled with contaminants, but we must live pure lives, maintaining ourselves as separate from all the corruption surrounding us. The Lord did not take us out of this world; rather, he interceded for us, asking God to protect us from the evil one (John 17:15). Following this request, Jesus asked the Father to "sanctify them by the truth," adding, "Your Word is truth" (John 17:17-19). This is the secret. The Word sanctifies us when it convicts us regarding righteousness, making us conscious of any contaminating sin in our lives. The Word helps us to appreciate God's holiness and to recognize our own condition before him.

Perhaps the Bible pictures this need for continual cleansing most powerfully in the story of the Lord washing the disciples' feet on the night he was betrayed (John 13:1-14). At first, Peter did not want to let the Lord do this precious work for him; it was, after all, a servant's work. The Lord told Peter that if he did not allow him to do this for him, Peter could have no part in him. Hearing this, enthusiastic Peter wanted a general wash! Then the Lord said, "A person who has had a bath needs only to wash his feet; his whole body is clean. And you are clean, though not every one of you" (John 13:10). In those days, with no running water in the houses, the people bathed in rivers or special water fountains and tanks set aside for this purpose. Returning home along dusty unpaved roads, they dirtied their sandaled feet, so the custom was to wash their feet when they got home. Having already had a bath, all they needed to wash was their feet.

It is clear that this story speaks of continual cleansing. Jesus describes people who have had a bath but later need to wash their feet again. Those who have had a bath are the believers, those who have been "washed in the blood of the Lamb." We know that Peter was a believer, and Jesus told him he was clean. We know that Judas was not a believer, despite the fact that he had walked with Jesus for three years, so Jesus said not all of them were clean. Jesus ties belief and "a bath" together here.

As the believer journeys home (to heaven) from the pool (life in the world), he gets his feet dirty. The believer must continually confess sin and be washed in Christ's blood for purification (1 John 1:7), though the continuous washing is not as extensive as the first. In this way, we maintain our communion with the Lord.

> If we confess our sins, he is faithful and just and will forgive us our sins and purify us from all unrighteousness (1 John 1:9).

This is the daily cleansing we need to practice that leads to our sanctification, or, in other words, to lives of holiness to the Lord. The Lord told the disciples that they would not understand what he was doing until later. He was showing his followers of all generations that the foot washing was a symbol of what he would continue to do in every period of the church's history.

Today the Lord cleanses us of all the contaminations of the world and of the sin that has entered our lives by applying the water of the Word to our lives. When we hear the voice of the Lord through his Word and we respond to it in our attitudes and actions, this refreshing water flows and removes all that defiles. When we continue in the Word, we are continually cleansed. This is a wondrous work of the Lord. "How can a young man keep his way pure? By living according to your word . . . I have hidden your word in my heart that I might not sin against you" (Psalm 119:9, 11).

The Combating Power of the Word

Beyond this need for continual cleansing, the believer also needs the Word to resist the enemy and to guide him. The weapon for both defense and attack is "the sword of the Spirit, which is the word of God" (Ephesians 6:17). God's sword is double-edged and can cut in two directions at the same time. It cuts forward to attack the enemy, and it cuts backward, convicting us as we turn it on ourselves, keeping us on the straight and narrow: "The word of God is living and active. Sharper than any double-edged sword, it penetrates even to dividing soul and spirit, joints and marrow; it judges the thoughts and attitudes of the heart" (Hebrews 4:12). It is a magnificent weapon! Like all warriors who live by their weapons, we must train well. If we do not exercise and use this sword, we will remain spiritually inexperienced and inefficient:

> Anyone who lives on milk, being still an infant, is not acquainted with the teaching about righteousness. But solid food is for the mature, who by constant use have trained themselves to distinguish good from evil. Therefore let us leave the elementary teachings about Christ and go on to maturity (Hebrews 5:13; 6:1).

Many passages speak of the Word of God containing milk for spiritual babes, the "newborn" in God's family. First Peter 2:2-3 and 1 Corinthians 3:1-2 speak to this aspect of the Word. We must begin with milk, basic doctrines; then we can progress to more difficult teaching, the meat that we need to gain strength to resist the enemy. First John 2:14 says, "I write to you, young men, because you are strong, and *the Word of God lives in you*, and you have overcome the evil one" (italics added) When we are firmly established in God's Word we will have a worthy weapon with which to resist the enemy.

When Satan tempted the Lord Jesus he resisted each temptation by using Scripture, beginning each response with, "It is written" (Matthew 4:1-11). The Lord's example demonstrates how to use the Word as an effective tool in gaining victory over temptation

---

and sin. Often we ask ourselves why we fall into sin so easily. Quite possibly, the reason is that we are not abiding in the Word, nor is it abiding in us. We have been promised a fruitful life for the Lord if we fulfill these two conditions:

> If you remain in me and my words remain in you, ask whatever you wish, and it will be given you. This is to my Father's glory, that you bear much fruit, showing yourselves to be my disciples (John 15:7-8).

We see that one of the requirements of receiving spiritual blessing is to not only know the Lord's commands, but to practice them. This is also a demonstration of our love of Christ. "Whoever has my commands and obeys them, he is the one who loves me. . . . If anyone loves me, he will obey my teaching. My Father will love him, and we will come to him and make our home with him" (John 14:21, 23).

Satan is attacking the church today by adulterating the Word. Paul mentions this practice in his second letter to the Corinthians:

> We have renounced the things hidden because of shame, not walking in craftiness or *adulterating the word of God*, but by the manifestation of truth, commending ourselves to every man's conscience in the sight of God (2 Corinthians 4:2, NASB, italics added).

Milkmen adulterate the milk they sell when they add water to it. A poor country farmer in Colombia once told me how his neighbor would add creek water to the ten gallon can of milk he sold to the milk company if he fell short. Those cans of milk were contaminated, adulterated. Milk is a basic food, especially for new babies, but when impure water is added, the food is weakened, and who knows how many parasites and other impurities have infected it. Satan wants to adulterate the Word by adding that which weakens: false doctrines, distortion, and deception. When he does this, he weakens the Word's power. Paul could say that he preached the Word in all purity:

We have renounced secret and shameful ways [those which are Satan's]; we do not use deception, nor do we distort the word of God (2 Corinthians 4:2).

The Capacitating Power of the Word

In 1 Timothy 3 we learn that the Lord has appointed the church to support and uplift truth, referring to the church as "the pillar and foundation of the truth" (1 Timothy 3:15). This shows us that we have a duty to defend the truth of the Word, and to do this it is essential that we know it well. "Do your best to present yourself to God as one approved, a workman who does not need to be ashamed and who correctly handles the word of truth" (2 Timothy 2:15). Paul exhorted Timothy to persist in the study of the Word, for in it he would find all that he would need to deal with matters relating to salvation and the Christian life. It would serve him to teach, to rebuke, to correct, and to train in righteousness. He had to persevere in it so that he would become a "man of God" who was "thoroughly equipped for every good work" (2 Timothy 3:15-17). Paul also exhorted Timothy to "preach the Word . . . correct, rebuke and encourage—with great patience and careful instruction. For the time will come when men will not put up with sound doctrine . . . they will turn away from the truth" (2 Timothy 4:2-4).

Ezra, the scribe and priest, is a good example of one who lived in the Word, and the Word in him. He "was a teacher well versed in the Law of Moses" (Ezra 7:6). According to Jewish tradition, Ezra would have known the Mosaic books by heart. He was the moving force in establishing the religious life of the Jews when they returned to Jerusalem from their captivity in Babylon. Ezra first prepared his heart by devoting himself "to the study and observance of the Law of the Lord, and to teaching its decrees and laws in Israel" (Ezra 7:10). Note the order used in applying the Word. First he applied it to his own heart, so that he was entirely prepared to obey and practice what it taught him. Only then could he teach others the ways of God with power and authority.

Take note of the authority by which the servants of God spoke in the Bible. What was their secret? They were propounding the word of God! "This is what the Lord says . . ." was the way many of their messages began, and as such it is our authority today as well. We should never think of ourselves as an authority or superior to others because of our education and training. Rather, we should recognize the fact that we are just servants and messengers whose authority comes from the Word of God.

Our Need for God's Continuous "Water" Supply

No one can live without water; the Water Gate in Jerusalem was, therefore, continually in use. *We* must continually use the Water Gate also, for it is impossible to successfully live for the Lord if we are not studying and applying the refreshing waters of the Word of God to our lives daily.

In closing, notice something interesting about the Water Gate: there is no mention of repairs being necessary to the gate itself. Nehemiah spoke of repairs *up to* the gate. This illustrates the fact that the Word of God is perfect and complete. Nothing need be added to it or taken from it. The Word will stand for eternity. Matthew records this powerful statement from the lips of our Lord: "Heaven and earth will pass away, but my words will never pass away" (Matthew 24:35).

THE HORSE GATE

Nehemiah 3:28

The Horse Gate, the eighth gate in Jerusalem's wall, was the main point of coming and going for Jerusalem's fighting forces. It was strategically situated near the king's palace, allowing the army to rapidly receive orders in times of emergency and then leave quickly by the main roads out of the city. It was most likely named the Horse Gate in the days of King Solomon, who stabled his vast herd of horses near this gate.

The Nature of the Battle and the Name of our Enemy

The Horse Gate speaks to us of Christian warfare and our need to stand firmly while facing the enemy. Just as the stables and soldiers were garrisoned near the king's palace, so we should station ourselves close to our leader, the Lord Jesus, so that we, like the cavalry of that day, can receive his orders and be prepared to obey them promptly.

The Horse Gate, symbolizing warfare, was located after the Water Gate, which speaks of the refining, cleansing power of the Word of God. When believers submit to the truth of the Word, Satan immediately begins to attack, seeking a way to disable the children of God and turn them away from the truth. The enemy does not want us to obey God. He himself refuses to submit to his Creator. Although Satan's profound hatred of us manifests itself in our lives as conflicts, trials, temptations, strife, and persecution, these attacks should also bring us into a place of victory and spiritual growth. Romans 5:3 says, "We also rejoice in our sufferings, because we know that suffering produces perseverance; perseverance, character; and character, hope."

In James 1:2-4 we read:

> Consider it pure joy, my brothers, whenever you face trials of many kinds, because you know that the testing of your faith develops perseverance. Perseverance must finish its work so that you may be mature and complete, not lacking anything.

Just as fire tempers iron, so trials are useful to foster the believer's growth. Trials help the believer, not to put his trust in himself, but to depend entirely on the Lord.

Satan's Battle Strategy against the Individual

Let's take a closer look at the nature of the enemy's battle strategy. First, we know that the attacks will be personal. We see an example of the personal nature of Satan's attacks in the familiar story of the Lord's temptation in the desert after his baptism (Matthew 4:1-11). In his perfect humanity, the Lord felt the weight of all these attacks, but he did not give in to them, and he never sinned.

> For we do not have a high priest who is unable to sympathize with our weaknesses, but we have one who has been tempted in every way, just as we are—yet was without sin (Hebrews 4:15).

At this present time, Jesus himself is interceding for us at the right hand of God. There is a Man in glory who can empathize with us when we face different kinds of trials and attacks from our enemy.

The devil attacked the human nature of the Lord while he was in a severely weakened state. He suggested that he make bread out of stones when the Lord was hungry after fasting for forty days. Satan also tempted him regarding his identity. "Are you really the Son of God?" was the question underlying the temptation to throw himself down from the temple. Satan tried to put doubts in his mind about God's care of him, and he tempted Jesus to do something carnal to reveal to others who he was. But the time was not right for the Lord to reveal himself. After this, Satan offered him power, fame, position, and sovereignty over the world—but on condition that the Lord bowed down and worshiped him. As we noted in the previous chapter, Jesus answered all these temptations with Scripture. This is where our victory is found as well.

Although Satan often attacks through our circumstances, many of his attacks will be focused in the mind. Satan knows well and is experienced in causing us to have doubts. Uneasiness, preoccupations, worries, tensions, evil thoughts, hate, selfishness, pride, fear, and all the desires of the flesh start in the mind: Let's take a closer

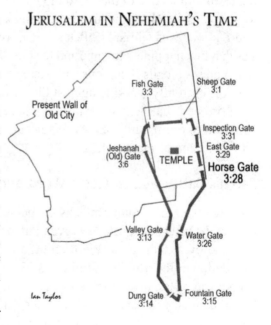

JERUSALEM IN NEHEMIAH'S TIME

Fish Gate 3:3

Sheep Gate 3:1

Present Wall of Old City

Inspection Gate 3:31

Jeshanah (Old) Gate 3:6

East Gate 3:29

TEMPLE

Horse Gate 3:28

Valley Gate 3:13

Water Gate 3:26

Ian Taylor

Dung Gate 3:14

Fountain Gate 3:15

look at the inwardly generated aspect of the sins listed in 1 John 2:15-16, which reads:

> Do not love the world or anything in the world. If anyone loves the world, the love of the Father is not in him. For everything in the world—the cravings of sinful man, the lust of his eyes and the boasting of what he has and does— comes not from the Father but from the world.

The lust of the flesh and the lust of the eyes comprise the desire to take possession of all that can be seen. Materialism, sexual immorality, and covetousness are all examples of lust of the eyes. All these desires feed greed, corruption, and moral degeneration. The boastful pride of life is the obsession with fame, position, and power. How many believers have sacrificed their spiritual lives on the altar of fame, power, and position to gain what this world considers important! But in the end they find that they have chased after the mist (James 4:14). The prevalence of this form of idolatry stems not only from Satan's shrewdness but also from a lack of knowledge of the Word of God and of the Lord himself. When we, instead, "grow in the grace and knowledge of our Lord and Savior Jesus Christ" (2 Peter 3:18), we can see through the lies that link happiness to fame and fortune. The NASB translation of 1 Peter 5:8 calls Satan our "adversary." Let us not doubt that Satan is currently working against the believer who is living for the Lord and that he is an expert at what he does. He has great insight into our natural desires. We need to resist him so that he will flee from us (James 4:7).

Satan's Battle against God's Word and the Church

We have seen that Satan's attacks are personal and often involve the mind. On a larger scale, however, Satan works to attack sound doctrine by assailing the Word and the church, the "pillar and foundation of the truth" (1 Timothy 3:15). The church, just like a supporting pillar, must uphold the truth and defend it as the first line of defense against the "father of lies." Satan's only weapon is the lie; our "only" weapon is the truth found in the Word of God.

The apostles spoke on many occasions about the enemies of Christ who would try to undermine the truth of God's Word. "The Spirit clearly says that in later times some will abandon the faith and follow deceiving spirits and things taught by demons" (1 Timothy 4:1). They spoke of deceitful men who would enter the church as though they were truly children of God. Instead, they were really emissaries of Satan, sent to sow lying doctrines and cause the destruction of the church. In 2 Timothy, Paul speaks of a moral degradation in the last days and the continued onslaught against truth:

> But mark this: There will be terrible times in the last days. People will be lovers of themselves, lovers of money, boastful, proud, abusive, disobedient to their parents, ungrateful, unholy, without love, unforgiving, slanderous, without self-control, brutal, not lovers of the good, treacherous, rash, conceited, lovers of pleasure rather than lovers of God—having a form of godliness but denying its power (2 Timothy 3:1-5).

John spoke of false prophets: "Dear friends, do not believe every spirit, but test the spirits to see whether they are from God, because many false prophets have gone out into the world" (1 John 4:1). "Spirits," here, refers to those who teach. In Acts 20:28-30, Paul warned the elders of the church at Ephesus that they should guard themselves and "all the flock over which the Holy Spirit has made [them] overseers." He continued: "Be shepherds of the church of God, which he bought with his own blood. I know that after I leave, savage wolves will come in among you and will not spare the flock. Even from your own number men will arise and distort the truth in order to draw away disciples after them."

Jude spoke strongly against godless people that change God's grace into a license for immorality, denying God and trying to destroy the Lord's work. For this reason, he said, we must "contend for the faith that was once entrusted to the saints" (Jude 3). The Christian life is a life of combat. We are soldiers of the faith and we must be ready and prepared for battle.

Our Equipment: Spiritual Armor and Weapons

The believer has provisions for the warfare, armor and weapons that are more than sufficient for our protection and the defense of the faith. Ephesians 6:10-18 details the various elements of the Christian armor and tells us how they are to be used. Paul encourages his readers to "be strong in the Lord and in his mighty power" (Ephesians 6:10). This is where we start. In the presence of the Lord we get to know him better, we enjoy fellowship with him, and we receive his power—the power of the Holy Spirit—in our lives.

We then have to put on the whole armor. This means that we have to wear it. It is a proactive action, requiring initiative and effort. We have to prepare ourselves and we have to put the armor on *fully* so that we can resist in the battle (Ephesians 6:11). If we do not have it all in place, we will have weak spots, vulnerable places that the devil will use to defeat us.

Ephesians 6:12-13 explains that our battle is not against flesh and blood but against spiritual hosts.

> For our struggle is not against flesh and blood, but against the rulers, against the authorities, against the powers of this dark world and against the spiritual forces of evil in the heavenly realms.

In other words, our battle is against the fallen spirits (demons) and Satan himself. Knowing this, it is very sad to see Christians fighting Christians instead of standing united to fight against our common enemy.

Lord Nelson, Admiral of the British Fleet, once discovered two of his officers quarreling. He approached, took them by the shoulders, and turned them about so that they both could see the Spanish fleet. Then he said, "Gentlemen, there is the enemy!" Instigating quarrels among believers has been one of Satan's most effective strategies. Our battle is not with men, and even less with our brothers in Christ; rather, it is against Satan and his hosts.

Paul goes on to say: "After you have done everything, stand" (v. 13). We see that the armor provides nothing for the back; we, therefore, must face the enemy and not flee from him, resisting the devil so that *he* will flee from *us*.

The Belt

"Stand firm then, with the belt of truth buckled around your waist" (v. 14). In biblical times, people wore long tunics that reached almost to the ground. To prevent a tunic from impeding you on a long trip or during a race, it was easier to attach it to a belt, freeing the legs from hindrances and entanglements. The Israelites, on the night of the Passover, were instructed to be ready to depart on their journey to Canaan with their cloaks tucked into their belts. The belt of truth subdues and removes the hindrances of falsehood, the deceptions the enemy has sown in this world. Again, truth is our foundation for all we do here. Let us leave all falsehood, sin, and weights behind, so that we can walk as children of light in a manner worthy of the Lord. Hebrews exhorts us to throw off everything that hinders so that we can run the race set out for us with all perseverance (Hebrews 12:1-2).

The Breastplate

"With the breastplate of righteousness in place" (v. 14). The breastplate is one of the largest pieces of armor. It protects the chest area—the heart—which is the place of our affections. Our righteousness in Christ must be visible. Not only are we now counted righteous "in Christ," but we also have the capacity to *live* righteously—in the power of the Spirit. Are we manifesting the righteousness of God in our lives? In our business? With our friends? If we truly love the Lord as we should, the change in our lives will be as evident as the breastplate on a soldier.

The Shoes

"And with your feet fitted with the readiness that comes from the gospel of peace" (v. 15). What a privilege to be the ones chosen to announce the good news to the lost! It is not only a privilege but an obligation. Paul said, "Woe to me if I do not preach the gospel" (1 Corinthians 9:16). The Lord has commissioned every believer to be a witness, wherever he is (Acts 1:8). Whenever we have the opportunity, we should use it—handing out tracts, witnessing to others as the opportunity arises, and doing the work of an evangelist. "How beautiful on the mountains are the feet of those who bring good news, who proclaim peace, who bring good tidings, who proclaim salvation" (Isaiah 52:7).

The Shield

"In addition to all this, take up the shield of faith, with which you can extinguish all the flaming arrows of the evil one" (v. 16). Faith is like a shield that provides a covering over all. Satan cannot defeat the believer who lives by faith. Many believers live by sight. They trust in their emotions or in other believers instead of looking at Christ and leaning on the Word of God and its promises. When Christians do not feel joyful, or when illnesses or trials come, instead of trusting and standing firm, these believers get discouraged and their spiritual life grows weak. When we live by faith, trusting fully in the Lord and in his Word, it does not matter when difficulties or trials come; we will go on. Our changing life situations and emotional states will not make any difference. We know that the Lord is the same "yesterday, today, and forever." We should not trust in ourselves for anything. He is all, he is faithful, and he is sufficient for us. Because He has promised to care and provide for us, let us put all our trust in him. "Blessed is the man who takes refuge in him" (Psalm 34:8).

The Helmet

"Take the helmet of salvation" (v. 17). The helmet protects the head. Linking salvation to the helmet shows how important it is for us to *understand* our salvation. A firm understanding of the doctrine of salvation will not only aid us immensely in witnessing to others but will shore up our defense against the enemy. Satan often tries to discourage us by sowing seeds of doubt that we are truly saved. Our salvation is secure when we trust in Christ as our only and all-sufficient Savior. When these discouragements come, it is time to look to Christ with the eye of faith and continue believing in him who is faithful.

The helmet returns us to the notion that Satan wants to destroy us through planting evil thoughts. If we have difficulties with the battle of the mind, we must find ways to overcome these attacks in the Word. In Philippians, we learn that we can take over lost mental ground by focusing our minds on profitable things: "Whatever is true, whatever is noble, whatever is right, whatever is pure, whatever is lovely, whatever is admirable—if anything is excellent or praiseworthy—think about such things" (Philippians 4:8).

To resist is active and positive; it is proactively filling our minds with what is worthwhile. If we are living a lie, practicing hypocrisy, it is time to think on what is true, and—above all—on him who *is* truth (John 14:6). If we struggle with evil thoughts concerning members of the opposite sex, or if pornography is a problem, we must occupy our minds with something that is decent and pure in order to clean them up. If our business dealings are of a doubtful nature, if we use devious tricks to gain a few cents, we must think about ways to put them right. If our thoughts towards others are malicious, we must concentrate on what is kind and good and reject what is bad. We must try to see what is virtuous in others and not criticize other believers. We should praise what is good in others and not degenerate into gossips. Above all, we should meditate on the righteous One who will judge all things done here on earth at the judgment seat of Christ (1 Corinthians 3:13; 2 Corinthians 5:10). Our minds are battlefields, and most of the victories are won there through self-control and a life subjected to the Lord.

> For though we live in the world, we do not wage war as the world does. The weapons we fight with are not the weapons of the world. On the contrary, they have divine power to demolish strongholds. We demolish arguments

and every pretension that sets itself up against the knowledge of God, and we take captive every thought to make it obedient to Christ (2 Corinthians 10:3-5).

The Sword

"The sword of the Spirit, which is the Word of God" (v. 17). This is the only weapon mentioned with which to attack Satan and defend ourselves. Every believer should exercise daily with this weapon until it is an intrinsic part of him or her and can be used with great ability. The Word is a very effective weapon!

Pray and Persevere

"And pray in the Spirit on all occasions with all kinds of prayer and requests. With this in mind, be alert and always keep on praying" (v. 18). Prayer is also an important part of the armor. The Word contains many promises concerning prayer, and they all show that God is always listening to the entreaties of his own children.

The battle intensifies every day because Satan can see that his time is running out. In these last days before the Lord's return, we must use the Horse Gate with greater frequency. The battle against the spiritual hosts is increasing. It is not the time to faint, nor is it time to get discouraged. We must remain firm and ready to defend our faith, resisting the devil in all that he does against the Lord and his church. With the help of the Lord we can all say, "No, in all these things we are more than conquerors through him who loved us" (Romans 8:37).

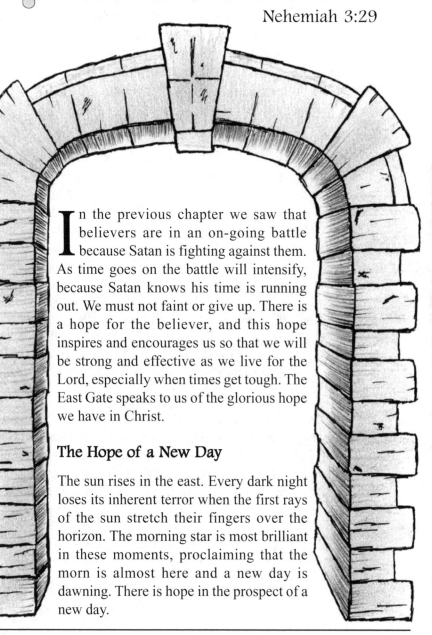

THE EAST GATE

Nehemiah 3:29

I n the previous chapter we saw that believers are in an on-going battle because Satan is fighting against them. As time goes on the battle will intensify, because Satan knows his time is running out. We must not faint or give up. There is a hope for the believer, and this hope inspires and encourages us so that we will be strong and effective as we live for the Lord, especially when times get tough. The East Gate speaks to us of the glorious hope we have in Christ.

The Hope of a New Day

The sun rises in the east. Every dark night loses its inherent terror when the first rays of the sun stretch their fingers over the horizon. The morning star is most brilliant in these moments, proclaiming that the morn is almost here and a new day is dawning. There is hope in the prospect of a new day.

Scripture provides insight into what kind of "hope" the East Gate represents. Through the prophet Ezekiel we learn that the East Gate represents the hope of the Messiah's return. In Ezekiel's vision (43:1-6) the prophet saw the glory of God enter through this gate to inhabit his future home. When Christ returns to reign he will arrive at the Mount of Olives, which is located in front of the East Gate. He will cross the valley, passing by the old Garden of Gethsemane, and will enter Jerusalem through the East Gate. This is the prophecy Ezekiel gave concerning this gate's very special purpose:

> Then the man brought me back to the outer gate to the sanctuary, the one facing east, and it was shut. The Lord said to me, "This gate is to remain shut. It must not be opened; no one may enter through it. It is to remain shut because the Lord, the God of Israel, has entered through it. The prince himself is the only one who may sit inside the gateway to eat in the presence of the Lord. He is to enter by way of the portico of the gateway and go out the same way" (Ezekiel 44:1-3).

True to the prophecy, this gateway is blocked up today with huge stones. No one can enter through it. The Jews will open it to receive their Messiah when he returns with his bride. Christ's reign will then commence and will last for a thousand years, and we will reign with him (Revelation 20:6)!

Through the prophet Malachi, God promised, "But for you who revere my name, the sun of righteousness will rise with healing in its wings" (Malachi 4:2). Peter said we should pay attention to prophetic words, for they are as "a light shining in a dark place, until the day dawns and the morning star rises in your hearts" (2 Peter 1:19).

These Scriptures comfort us, for we know that the dark night of the Son's absence is passing, and dawn will soon arrive. There are signs that this dawn is near. When our Lord appears, we will spend eternity with him.

A Promise that Inspires Hope

On the night he was betrayed, Jesus gave a prophecy to inspire hope in his followers that they would need after his death, resurrection, and ascension into heaven. "Do not let your hearts be troubled. Trust in God; trust also in me. In my Father's house are many rooms; if it were not so, I would have told you. I am going there to prepare a place for you. And if I go and prepare a place for you, *I will come back and take you to be with me that you also may be where I am"* (John 14:1-3, italics added).

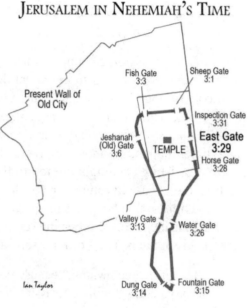

JERUSALEM IN NEHEMIAH'S TIME

Fish Gate 3:3
Sheep Gate 3:1
Present Wall of Old City
Inspection Gate 3:31
Jeshanah (Old) Gate 3:6
TEMPLE
East Gate 3:29
Horse Gate 3:28
Valley Gate 3:13
Water Gate 3:26
Dung Gate 3:14
Fountain Gate 3:15
Ian Taylor

Angels confirmed this promise as the Lord was taken up to heaven. While his disciples stood gazing after him, they said: "Men of Galilee, why do you stand here looking into the sky? This same Jesus, who has been taken from you into heaven, will come back in the same way you have seen him go into heaven" (Acts 1:11). These were truly comforting words for the disciples! They never forgot what they had been told and lived in anticipation of the return of their Lord and Savior.

During the first persecutions by the Romans, when believers were assigned to the lions or to death at the hands of gladiators in the Coliseum, many martyrs wrote a single word of encouragement on the walls of their cells to encourage and comfort others who would follow them. The word was "MARANATHA," which means "OUR LORD COMES!" This was a truly inspiring word that gave courage and strength to all of those martyrs who gave their lives for the Lord. The apostle Paul used the word "Maranatha" as a farewell to the Corinthians in his first letter to them (1 Corinthians 16:22).

Some of the Thessalonian believers had quit their jobs, thinking that the Lord's return was so imminent that they did not need to keep on working. This was never the idea, and Paul told them plainly: "If a man shall not work, he shall not eat" (2 Thessalonians 3:10). We must live as though Christ might return today. At the same time, though, we must be practical; we must plan, work, and live, as though he might not return for years. No one knows the time the Lord will return for his church. The Word is silent about the time so that believers in all ages will live each day with hope, having their lives in order and serving with diligence during the time given them. The Lord himself said,

> Therefore keep watch, because you do not know on what day your Lord will come (Matthew 24:42).

The Lord's Return *for* His Church

The Bible speaks of the Lord returning two times, the first to collect his bride (the church), the second to reign with his bride on the earth. First Thessalonians provides teaching concerning this first coming, called the rapture of the church (4:13-17). Some Thessalonians, not understanding the doctrine of the Lord's return, were distressed because they thought that believing loved ones who had died would not participate in the rapture. Paul wrote to comfort them. He taught that those who had accepted the Lord as Savior during their lives were not annihilated at death, but were merely "asleep" in Christ. It is *the Lord himself* who will come. He will not send an angel or any other messenger for his bride; rather, he will come in person to receive her. This coming will be announced with "a shout." It will surely be a triumphant shout, for the time will have come for him to be literally united with his chosen people. Only those who belong to him will hear his voice. Those who are not saved will miss the call.

Along with the archangel's call, God's trumpet will sound as the Lord returns. Trumpets were often used as instruments of battle. Soldiers advanced or retreated depending on the tune played. On that day even the *dead* in Christ will hear the trumpet blast. The Lord will descend and the dead in Christ will rise first. There should be no fear of dying in Christ because the Lord, through his resurrection, has taken away death's sting (1 Corinthians 15:55-57). He rose as the first fruits from among the dead; in other words, he was the first of millions who will also one day rise again (1 Corinthians 15:20-23). How long will it take for our resurrected, corruptible bodies to be transformed into glorified and incorruptible bodies?

> In a flash, in the twinkling of an eye, at the last trumpet. For the trumpet will sound, the dead will be raised imperishable, and we will be changed (1 Corinthians 15:52).

Those of us who are still alive when the Lord returns "will be caught up with them in the clouds to meet the Lord in the air. And so we will be with the Lord forever" (1 Thessalonians 4:17). What a hope for believers! We shall be removed from earthly trials, sin, problems, persecutions, prejudices, and we will be with the Lord forever!

Notice that this is a secret encounter, only for the church. The unbelieving world will remain on earth to experience different forms of terrible judgments. The book of Revelation, starting from chapter 6, foretells these horrible events that will befall those who will be left behind.

Recognizing that the Lord could return at any moment to collect his bride, how should we live? The apostle John said: "And now, dear children, continue in him, so that when he appears we may be confident and unashamed before him at his coming. . . . And everyone who has this hope in him purifies himself, just as he is pure" (1 John 2:28; 3:3). From these verses we understand that it is possible for believers to feel shame at the Lord's return if they are living in a manner that is not worthy of him.

The Lord related several parables emphasizing the need for diligence while we wait for his return. We need to be trustworthy regarding his interests while we wait. We should be alert so that his return will not surprise us. While the parable of the ten virgins is mainly directed at the nation of Israel, the main point of the illustration shows that the coming of the Lord will find people who are not prepared or ready (Matthew 25:1-13). What applied to Israel then, applies to us today. The parable closes with these words: "Therefore keep watch, because you do not know the day or the hour" (Matthew 25:13).

In the parable of the talents (Matthew 25:14-30), the main principle concerns what we are doing with the gifts and abilities the Lord has given us while we wait for him. We are responsible to use our time, belongings, and capabilities diligently in service to the Lord, so that we will not be ashamed when he returns for his church.

The Lord's Return *with* His Church

There has been some confusion concerning the Lord's return *for* his church and the Lord's return *with* his church. The first coming is a secret one, and only true believers will participate in it. This first reappearance will be the reunion between the *Lord* and his *bride*, and on that occasion, he will not return to the earth but will meet her (the church) in the air (1 Thessalonians 4:17).

After the rapture of the church, the tribulation will begin here on the earth (prophesied by Daniel and the Lord himself). The tribulation will last about seven years (Daniel 9:25-27; Matthew 24:9-22). The events of the tribulation are explained in Revelation chapters 6-19 and in Matthew 24. At the end of that time, the Lord Jesus will return to the earth to establish his kingdom and to save Israel, his people of old. At that time the prophecies made about the land of Israel and the nation of Israel will be fulfilled. These promises were originally given to Abraham (Genesis 12), were confirmed to the other patriarchs, and were later confirmed to King David and his descendants (2 Samuel 7). All these promises will eventually be fulfilled.

Revelation 19 instructs us concerning the return of the Lord *with* the church. It speaks of his return with the heavenly hosts. The main difference about this return is that *everyone will see him.* He will come to the earth, where he will fight in Israel's favor against the Beast, the False Prophet, and the evil hosts: "For as lightning that comes from the east is visible even in the west, so will be the coming of the Son of Man" (Matthew 24:27). "And then the lawless one will be revealed, whom the Lord Jesus will overthrow with the breath of his mouth and destroy by the splendor of his coming" (2 Thessalonians 2:8). It is at *this* coming that Christ will fulfill Ezekiel's prophecy and enter Jerusalem through the East Gate, the triumphant King of kings.

Our Hope

We should never lose hope, even when we pass through the most difficult circumstances of life. When the going gets rough, remember: "MARANATHA!" The Lord is coming! After this short life has passed, we will spend eternity together with him. What a wonderful hope!

THE INSPECTION GATE

Nehemiah 3:31

The name *Miphkad*, the Hebrew name of the final gate, has been translated in several different ways. Some translators opt to transliterate the Hebrew rather than determine an English equivalent. The NIV translators chose "Inspection Gate"; the NRSV translates the name as "Muster Gate," a place of review; and the KJV uses the Hebrew "gate Miphkad." Some think Miphkad was a house of visitation or correction, while others consider it the place where the Sanhedrin sat and tried cases. Another commentator describes this gate as "the place of judgment or execution." All seem to agree that *Miphkad* speaks of an area leading to the place where some kind of judgment was meted out. We will use "Inspection Gate" to emphasize this "judgment" aspect of the word, as this seems to be the best translation in relation to the progression we have seen in the other nine gates of Nehemiah's time.

A Future Inspection Based on the Life Lived Now

As we reach the Inspection Gate, we have almost made the complete trip around the city of Jerusalem. We have seen the names, the order, and the spiritual implications of each gate. The previous gate, the East Gate, speaks of the believers' hope in the return of the Lord Jesus and his reign with his church from Jerusalem. With this in mind, we see that the spiritual dimensions of the Inspection Gate relate to events that will take place *after* the Lord's return. The Inspection Gate represents the coming judgment where all believers' works will be reviewed. Knowledge of this judgment gives us reason to stand firm, persevere, and live diligently for Christ. What will happen to us after death, or after the Lord's return, depends entirely on what we do for him now while we are on earth.

That the Inspection Gate primarily speaks about the judgment of the saints is supported by another aspect of historical deduction concerning this gate. Some have postulated that, in addition to being the place where the Sanhedrin may have tried cases, the Inspection Gate may also have been the place where the troops were inspected or reviewed. This helps us understand what kind of judgment was made there. Rather than simply being a place for deciding guilt or innocence, this gate witnessed captains inspecting the troops to decide whether each soldier had fulfilled certain duties.

In the same way, believers (those already shown to be innocent by virtue of Christ's blood and who count themselves as members of the Lord's army) will stand before the Lord. He will decide how well we have fulfilled our Christian duties. "When the roll is called up yonder"—in heaven, that is—we will be able to say "Present!" Then we will receive the rewards won while serving the Lord on earth: "Command them to do good, to be rich in good deeds, and to be generous and willing to share. In this way they will lay up treasure for themselves as a firm foundation for the coming age, so that they may take hold of the life that is truly life" (1 Timothy 6:18-19).

Again, read the verse from Ephesians we studied earlier: "Put on the full armor of God, so that when the day of evil comes, you may be able to stand your ground, and after you have done everything, to stand" (Ephesians 6:13).

Knowing that the judgment seat of Christ is before us, we should live our lives in such a way that we show we are ready for the inspection and have no fear of the Lord's arrival. A well-prepared soldier who wants to please his commanding officer will not only always be ready for action but can hope for promotions and honors (2 Timothy 2:4).

Of course, the Inspection Gate implies another kind of inspection. Before we are reviewed by a superior, we take the time to inspect ourselves. A Christian must constantly practice "self-inspection" to make sure his life is constantly in tune with God. We not only have to put on the whole armor of God; we are also to be clean (with pure lives), and well nourished (in the Word) so we will be ready to fulfill all the purposes the Lord has for us.

The Time, Nature, and Place of Judgment for the Unbeliever

The Word speaks of two main types of future judgment: the judgment of what the believer has done for his Lord and the judgment of those who are not saved. This latter judgment refers to those who will be condemned to eternal punishment. Though we have been applying each

JERUSALEM IN NEHEMIAH'S TIME

Present Wall of Old City

Fish Gate 3:3

Sheep Gate 3:1

Inspection Gate 3:31

Jeshanah (Old) Gate 3:6

TEMPLE

East Gate 3:29

Horse Gate 3:28

Valley Gate 3:13

Water Gate 3:26

Ian Taylor

Dung Gate 3:14

Fountain Gate 3:15

gate to the believer and the church, we should step aside for a minute and apply the Inspection Gate to the unbeliever, to those who, like Simon the sorcerer, have no "part or share in this ministry, because [their hearts are] not right before God" (Acts 8:21). Judgment for the unbeliever is described as the "Great White Throne judgment," where eternal punishment will be meted out to those who have never confessed Jesus Christ as their Redeemer.

I hope that, if you are reading this and are not saved, you will meditate on this section more than any other, for it is of utmost importance that you accept the salvation the Lord Jesus offers you while there is yet time. After death there will be no more opportunity, and your eternal destiny will be fixed. Read again the chapter on the Sheep Gate and begin using Jerusalem's Gates.

The Revelation 20:11-15 teaching about the Great White Throne judgment is quite clear:

> Then I saw a great white throne . . . And I saw the dead, great and small, standing before the throne, and books were opened. Another book was opened, which is the book of life. The dead were judged according to what they had done as recorded in the books. . . . If anyone's name was not found written in the book of life, he was thrown into the lake of fire.

No believer will have to stand before the Great White Throne, because they have acknowledged that Jesus Christ was judged for their sin on the cross. He was punished in our place, as Galatians 3:13 plainly states: "Christ redeemed us from the curse of the law by becoming a curse for us, for it is written: 'Cursed is everyone who is hung on a tree.'"

One thing is absolutely certain: those who have not received the Lord Jesus Christ as Savior while they live here on earth will have to stand in judgment before the Great White Throne, after which they will be judged and then thrown into the lake of fire for all eternity. "Just as it is appointed for mortals to die once, and after that the judgment" (Hebrews 9:27, NRSV). "For the wages of sin is death, but the gift of God is eternal life in Christ Jesus our Lord" (Romans 6:23). We have all sinned; and because of this we are all automatically condemned to hell, but God, in his great love, sent his only Son to die on the cross as a substitute for the sinner, making a way of escape. "For God so loved the world that he gave his one and only Son, that whoever believes in him shall not perish but have eternal life" (John 3:16).

Those who refuse this love offering are already condemned, even before appearing at the Great White Throne: "Whoever believes in him is not condemned, but whoever does not believe stands condemned already because he has not believed in the name of God's one and only Son" (John 3:18). The Great White Throne judgment *will* take place, and at that time the condemnation of all unbelievers will be applied. Accept Christ now while there's still time!

The Time, Nature, and Place of Judgment for the Believer

We will now look at how the Inspection Gate is applied to the believer in the spiritual context of this study. At Christ's return, the church will be caught up to heaven. Meanwhile, here on earth, the tribulation will begin. After our arrival in heaven, certain events will take place in which the redeemed will participate, as is prophesied in Revelation, starting with chapter 4. One of the first of these events will be the appearance of all believers before the Judgment Seat of Christ, "that each one may receive what is due him for the things done while in the body, whether good or bad" (2 Corinthians 5:10b).

Christ's judgment of the believers will not be a judgment of sin; rather, it will resemble the scene where a captain inspects his troops. Christ will reward each one according to their work done while on the earth. The "judgment seat," or *bema*, was the name of the platform used at the ancient Greek Olympic Games, upon which the winners were decorated. This was done in much the same way as in our times at the Olympic Games, when the gold, silver, and bronze medals are awarded. At the end of our journey, there will be rewards for service well done.

The Lord himself told several parables showing that the faithful servant will be rewarded for his work. As recorded in Luke 19:11-27, he told the parable of the ten minas and how the ten servants used them. The number ten speaks of responsibility and teaches us that each person has gifts from the Lord and is responsible before him for using them while he waits for the Lord's return. The first servant worked hard with what he had received from his lord, and he gained ten minas more. He and the other servants who served their lord well with their gifts were rewarded when their lord returned:

> Well done, my good servant! Because you have been trustworthy in a very small matter, take charge of ten cities (Luke 19:17).

In a similar parable recorded in Matthew 25:14-30, the Lord told of a man who had given money (called "talents") to three different men, each according to his abilities. After being far away for a time, he returned, and his servants had to give an accounting of what they had accomplished with the resources entrusted to them. Two had worked well and increased their talents, but the other hid his talent and was very ashamed when he had to face his master. Those who were faithful received their rewards. The one who did not use his talent suffered loss; he was accused of being negligent.

These two parables help us to understand that the Lord will reward all his faithful servants. In the first parable mentioned, each servant received the same initial number of minas. This teaches us that we all have the same opportunities to serve the Lord. In this sense, there is no reason for a person to say that there was nothing he could do for the Lord. In the second parable, each one received according to his abilities. This teaches us that we all have different gifts and abilities and we are responsible before the Lord as to how we use them. We must be faithful with what we have.

The truths about the way we work for the Lord, determining the quality of our service and the kinds of rewards we receive, is explained well in Paul's first letter to the Corinthians:

> So neither he who plants nor he who waters is anything, but only God, who makes things grow. The man who plants and the man who waters have one purpose, and each will be rewarded according to his own labor.... But each one should be careful how he builds. For no one can lay any foundation other than the one already laid, which is Jesus Christ. If any man builds on this foundation using gold, silver, costly stones, wood, hay or straw, his work will be shown for what it is, because the Day will bring it to light. It will be revealed with fire, and the fire will test the quality of each man's work. *If what he has built survives, he will receive his reward.* If it is burned up, he will suffer loss; he himself will be saved, but only as one escaping through the flames (1 Corinthians 3:7-8, 10-15, italics added).

When we work according to God's will and for the glory of his name, serving him acceptably, this service is likened to gold, silver, and precious stones. If we serve the Lord out of pride, selfishness, greed, or any other fleshly motive, we are heaping up "rewards" of wood, hay, and straw—materials that will burn up under God's scrutiny. Only what we do for Christ with right motives will last.

Encouragement for the Saint and Exaltation for the Savior

We should always remember that we are not competing against others. The Lord is not expecting more from us than what we are capable of doing, but neither will he be satisfied with less than we're able to do! The Christian must prepare and equip himself as much as possible so that he can do his "best to present [himself] to God as one approved, a workman who does not need to be ashamed" (2 Timothy 2:15).

Do not be discouraged, feeling that your talents are not of much value. God knows your capabilities because he made you. Your responsibility is to do your best. "Run in such a way as to get the prize. Everyone who competes in the games goes into strict training. They do it to get a crown that will not last; but we do it to get a crown that will last forever" (1 Corinthians 9:24-25).

The Bible speaks of several crowns that will be given to the faithful. What is the purpose of these crowns? Although they are prizes, there is an even better reason for them. We receive crowns so that we can eventually lay them at the Lord's feet. We receive crowns so that we can express our love for him. This is why we work for the Lord: because we love him, not because we want a heap of prizes or because we want to feel better than others in heaven. There will be no place in heaven for jealousies, pride, or any other feeling prompted by the flesh. When we stand before the Lord it will be our privilege to have something in our hands to place at the feet of the One who is worthy of all praise and glory:

> They lay their crowns before the throne and say: "You are worthy, our Lord and God, to receive glory and honor and power, for you created all things, and by your will they were created and have their being" (Revelation 4:10-11).

What a day that will be, when our glorious Lord and Savior will receive the adoration and the praise he deserves! It would be a great pity to not have something in our hands at that moment to offer him. This is the reason we work and serve the Lord with all diligence and faithfulness, knowing that this life will ultimately culminate in praise to God. "Blessed is that servant whose master finds him [working] when he returns" (Matthew 24:46).

The End of the Tour and the End of Time

In Nehemiah 3:32, after passing the Inspection Gate, the text comes again to the Sheep Gate. The circle is complete, and it ends as it began, with the Lamb of God before our eyes. He is the "Alpha and the Omega, the First and the Last, the Beginning and the End" (Revelation 22:13). He is the immutable one, Jesus Christ, "the same yesterday and today and forever" (Hebrews 13:8). In that day, when everything will be subject to him and his enemies will be placed under his feet, he will be "marveled at among all those who have believed" (2 Thessalonians 1:10), and we shall see him as "him who fills everything in every way" (Ephesians 1:23). In heaven the multitudes will sing the new song of glory to the Lamb (Revelation 5:9-10, 13). Our response should be, "Amen. Come, Lord Jesus."

NOTES

NOTES